JavaScript Domain-Driven Design

Speed up your application development by leveraging the patterns of domain-driven design

Philipp Fehre

BIRMINGHAM - MUMBAI

JavaScript Domain-Driven Design

First published: July 2015

Production reference: 1270715

Published by Packt Publishing Ltd.
Livery Place
35 Livery Street
Birmingham B3 2PB, UK.

ISBN 978-1-78439-432-5

www.packtpub.com

Credits

Author
Philipp Fehre

Reviewers
Vahagn Grigoryan
Max Kirchoff
Michael Smith

Commissioning Editor
Taron Pereira

Acquisition Editors
Sonali Vernekar
Greg Wild

Content Development Editor
Rohit Kumar Singh

Technical Editor
Rohith Rajan

Copy Editors
Charlotte Carneiro
Ameesha Smith-Green

Project Coordinator
Mary Alex

Proofreader
Safis Editing

Indexer
Tejal Soni

Graphics
Jason Monteiro

Production Coordinator
Melwyn D'sa

Cover Work
Melwyn D'sa

About the Author

Philipp Fehre is a software engineer, conference organizer, speaker, and educator. Having seen many different applications as a consultant, he moved on to educate developers as an advocate of the NoSQL technology and is now working as a backend software engineer. He has also been a writer for the German Linux magazine in the past.

For years, he has been fascinated by the possibilities of JavaScript and followed Node.js from its beginnings, using it for research projects and production web services.

I'd like to thank my wife, Steffi, for her continuous support and for dealing with me spending my nights writing this. I'd also like to thank the reviewers for doing an awesome job of finding all the places where I could have done better. I hope I did justice to their efforts.

About the Reviewers

Vahagn Grigoryan is a senior web developer who is currently working at Learnship Networks. He has more than 10 years of full-stack application development experience, ranging from LAMP to frontend RESTful applications. He has worked for companies such as Lycos and Telegate, and is currently working at Learnship Networks. This is the first book that he has reviewed. He is married and has a 2-year-old son.

> I'm happy to thank my parents for their consistent guidance and shiny presence on each step of my life.

Max Kirchoff built his first website in 1996 on a little hosting service called GeoCities. He was not only immediately fascinated by the ability to distribute information with a graphical interface, but was also frustrated with how difficult it was to do interesting things with those early web browsers. As time passed and the technology evolved, Max built more and more websites, eventually working as a consultant for e-commerce early adopter businesses and then with advertising agencies, building campaigns that were on the bleeding edge of the Web. Along the way, he has worked on everything from leading the implementation of service-oriented architecture to UX prototyping and a thousand things in between. JavaScript was never his favorite language, but after working with a friend who "loved JS," he also came around and saw the strength and flexibility it provided for building beautiful and powerful web applications.

Max currently works for Google, where he works closely with advertisment platform partners to inform and enhance their web interfaces for better user experience.

> I'd love to thank my grandmother, who was a brilliant and inspiring rebel who broke all the rules and challenged every thoughtless barrier anyone put in front of her.

Michael Smith is a developer and consultant with 15 years of experience. He has worked in a broad range of industries, including banking, finance, e-commerce, and oil. He is passionate about delivering high-quality software that actually meets and exceeds the client's needs. To this end, he is an advocate of putting the business front and center when developing software and exploring ways to encourage better communication between all stakeholders in a project.

He is involved in various open source projects, including a line of business application framework called Bifrost.

www.PacktPub.com

Support files, eBooks, discount offers, and more

For support files and downloads related to your book, please visit www.PacktPub.com.

Did you know that Packt offers eBook versions of every book published, with PDF and ePub files available? You can upgrade to the eBook version at www.PacktPub.com and as a print book customer, you are entitled to a discount on the eBook copy. Get in touch with us at service@packtpub.com for more details.

At www.PacktPub.com, you can also read a collection of free technical articles, sign up for a range of free newsletters and receive exclusive discounts and offers on Packt books and eBooks.

https://www2.packtpub.com/books/subscription/packtlib

Do you need instant solutions to your IT questions? PacktLib is Packt's online digital book library. Here, you can search, access, and read Packt's entire library of books.

Why subscribe?

- Fully searchable across every book published by Packt
- Copy and paste, print, and bookmark content
- On demand and accessible via a web browser

Free access for Packt account holders

If you have an account with Packt at www.PacktPub.com, you can use this to access PacktLib today and view 9 entirely free books. Simply use your login credentials for immediate access.

Instant updates on new Packt books

Get notified! Find out when new books are published by following @PacktEnterprise on Twitter or the *Packt Enterprise* Facebook page.

Table of Contents

Preface

Welcome to *JavaScript Domain-Driven Design*. For years, JavaScript has been stuck in the realm of making a website a little more interactive, but nobody would have thought about implementing whole applications in JavaScript. This has changed dramatically over the past few years, and JavaScript has evolved into this omnipresent powerhouse of a language that is present in almost every space of development.

This phenomenal growth has introduced many problems during development, which were previously unknown in the JavaScript world. Projects grow to very large codebases, many developers work simultaneously on these large codebases, and in the end, JavaScript is more often than not a vital part of the overall application. The good thing is that most of those problems have been solved before, and we, as JavaScript developers, can draw from the vast experiences gained over the years in other spaces and adapt them to work for us in JavaScript, leveraging JavaScript's unique flexibility along the way.

What this book covers

Chapter 1, A Typical JavaScript Project, introduces a typical business application and how it is developed. It shows how domain-driven design can help steer clear of common issues during the development to create a more problem-tailored application.

Chapter 2, Finding the Core Problem, shows how we can effectively explore an application's problem domain and identify the most important aspects to work on.

Chapter 3, Setting up a Project for Domain-driven Design, focuses on setting up a structure for the project that is ready to grow. It not only shows how we can lay out files and folders, but also creates the right testing and build environments.

Chapter 4, Modelling the Actors, shows how a project grows using object-oriented techniques together with domain-driven design to really isolate the domain. We also tackle one of the hardest problems of computer science, naming.

Chapter 5, Classification and Implementation, is all about the language we use in domain-driven design to make the project understandable and readable. We look at the relationship between domains and sub-domains, and then drill further down into the core of domain objects.

Chapter 6, Context Map – The Big Picture, is about not only growing the application from a technical perspective, but also from an organizational perspective. We talk about organizing the different parts that form the application as a whole, either as separate parts or as interlinked pieces.

Chapter 7, It's Not All Domain-driven Design, talks about fitting domain-driven design into the space of development techniques, talking about what problems fit where. We also talk about influences such as object-orientation, domain-specific languages, and more.

Chapter 8, Seeing It All Come Together, is about how our project fits into a space of projects in JavaScript, referring back to the beginning. We also look at alternative choices for frameworks and development styles.

What you need for this book

The book uses JavaScript as the language of choice throughout. In order to provide a consistent runtime environment, JavaScript Node.js is used throughout the book as the runtime. Other tools from the Node.js ecosystem are used as well, mainly npm as the package manager. To work with the code in the book, you need a version of Node.js, which is available for Windows, Macintosh OS, and Linux from the Node.js website `http://nodejs.org/`. It comes packaged with npm. For editing code, I recommend using your favorite text editor or IDE. If you don't have one, maybe give Sublime Text or Vim a try, these are also available for Windows, Macintosh OS, and Linux.

Who this book is for

This book assumes a certain familiarity with the JavaScript language. It is targeted at JavaScript developers, who are faced with the problems of growing applications, and the problems that arise from the growth. It provides a practical approach to domain-driven design and focuses on the parts that are the most useful in day-to-day development.

Conventions

In this book, you will find a number of text styles that distinguish between different kinds of information. Here are some examples of these styles and an explanation of their meaning.

Code words in text, database table names, folder names, filenames, file extensions, pathnames, dummy URLs, user input, and Twitter handles are shown as follows: "At the time of the writing, the currently active version was `node.js 0.10.33`."

A block of code is set as follows:

```
var Dungeon = function(cells) {
  this.cells = cells
  this.bookedCells = 0
}
```

When we wish to draw your attention to a particular part of a code block, the relevant lines or items are set in bold:

```
var dungeons = {}
Dungeon.find = function(id, callback) {
  if (!dungeons[id]) {
    dungeons[id] = new Dungeon(100)
  }
```

Any command-line input or output is written as follows:

```
$ npm install -g express
```

New terms and **important words** are shown in bold. Words that you see on the screen, for example, in menus or dialog boxes, appear in the text like this: "Clicking on the **Next** button moves you to the next screen."

Important links or important notes appear in a box like this.

Tips and tricks appear like this.

Reader feedback

Feedback from our readers is always welcome. Let us know what you think about this book—what you liked or disliked. Reader feedback is important for us as it helps us develop titles that you will really get the most out of.

To send us general feedback, simply e-mail `feedback@packtpub.com`, and mention the book's title in the subject of your message.

If there is a topic that you have expertise in and you are interested in either writing or contributing to a book, see our author guide at `www.packtpub.com/authors`.

Customer support

Now that you are the proud owner of a Packt book, we have a number of things to help you to get the most from your purchase.

Downloading the example code

You can download the example code files from your account at `http://www.packtpub.com` for all the Packt Publishing books you have purchased. If you purchased this book elsewhere, you can visit `http://www.packtpub.com/support` and register to have the files e-mailed directly to you.

Errata

Although we have taken every care to ensure the accuracy of our content, mistakes do happen. If you find a mistake in one of our books—maybe a mistake in the text or the code—we would be grateful if you could report this to us. By doing so, you can save other readers from frustration and help us improve subsequent versions of this book. If you find any errata, please report them by visiting `http://www.packtpub.com/submit-errata`, selecting your book, clicking on the **Errata Submission Form** link, and entering the details of your errata. Once your errata are verified, your submission will be accepted and the errata will be uploaded to our website or added to any list of existing errata under the Errata section of that title.

To view the previously submitted errata, go to `https://www.packtpub.com/books/content/support` and enter the name of the book in the search field. The required information will appear under the **Errata** section.

Piracy

Piracy of copyrighted material on the Internet is an ongoing problem across all media. At Packt, we take the protection of our copyright and licenses very seriously. If you come across any illegal copies of our works in any form on the Internet, please provide us with the location address or website name immediately so that we can pursue a remedy.

Please contact us at copyright@packtpub.com with a link to the suspected pirated material.

We appreciate your help in protecting our authors and our ability to bring you valuable content.

Questions

If you have a problem with any aspect of this book, you can contact us at questions@packtpub.com, and we will do our best to address the problem.

1

A Typical JavaScript Project

Welcome to domain-driven design in JavaScript. In this book, we will explore a practical approach to developing software with advanced business logic. There are many strategies to keep development flowing and the code and thoughts organized, there are frameworks building on conventions, there are different software paradigms such as object orientation and functional programming, or methodologies such as test-driven development. All these pieces solve problems, and are like tools in a toolbox to help manage growing complexity in software, but they also mean that today when starting something new, there are loads of decisions to make even before we get started at all. Do we want to develop a single-page application, do we want to develop following the standards of a framework closely or do we want to set our own? These kinds of decisions are important, but they also largely depend on the context of the application, and in most cases the best answer to the questions is: *it depends*.

So, how do we really start? Do we really even know what our problem is, and, if we understand it, does this understanding match that of others? Developers are very seldom the domain experts on a given topic. Therefore, the development process needs input from outside through experts of the business domain when it comes to specifying the behavior a system should have. Of course, this is not only true for a completely new project developed from the ground up, but also can be applied to any new feature added during development of to an application or product. So, even if your project is well on its way already, there will come a time when a new feature just seems to bog the whole thing down and, at this stage, you may want to think about alternative ways to go about approaching this new piece of functionality.

Domain-driven design gives us another useful piece to play with, especially to solve the need to interact with other developers, business experts, and product owners. As in the modern era, JavaScript becomes a more and more persuasive choice to build projects in and, in many cases like browser-based web applications, it actually is the only viable choice. Today, the need to design software with JavaScript is more pressing than ever. In the past, the issues of a more involved software design were focused on either backend or client application development, with the rise of JavaScript as a language to develop complete systems in, this has changed. The development of a JavaScript client in the browser is a complex part of developing the application as a whole, and so is the development of server-side JavaScript applications with the rise of **Node.js**. In modern development, JavaScript plays a major role and therefore needs to receive the same amount of attention in development practices and processes as other languages and frameworks have in the past. A browser based client-side application often holds the same amount, or even more logic, than the backend. With this change, a lot of new problems and solutions have arisen, the first being the movement toward better encapsulation and modularization of JavaScript projects. New frameworks have arisen and established themselves as the bases for many projects. Last but not least, JavaScript made the jump from being the language in the browser to move more and more to the server side, by means of Node.js or as the query language of choice in some **NoSQL** databases. Let me take you on a tour of developing a piece of software, taking you through the stages of creating an application from start to finish using the concepts domain-driven design introduced and how they can be interpreted and applied.

In this chapter, you will cover:

- The core idea of domain-driven design
- Our business scenario — managing an orc dungeon
- Tracking the business logic
- Understanding the core problem and selecting the right solution
- Learning what domain-driven design is

The core idea of domain-driven design

There are many software development methodologies around, all with pros and cons but all also have a core idea, which is to be applied and understood to get the methodology right. For a domain-driven design, the core lies in the realization that since we are not the experts in the domain the software is placed in, we need to gather input from other people who are experts. This realization means that we need to optimize our development process to gather and incorporate this input.

So, what does this mean for JavaScript? When thinking about a browser application to expose a certain functionality to a consumer, we need to think about many things, for example:

- How does the user expect the application to behave in the browser?
- How does the business workflow work?
- What does the user know about the workflow?

These three questions already involve three different types of experts: a person skilled in user experience can help with the first query, a business domain expert can address the second query, and a third person can research the target audience and provide input on the last query. Bringing all of this together is the goal we are trying to achieve.

While the different types of people matter, the core idea is that the process of getting them involved is always the same. We provide a common way to talk about the process and establish a quick feedback loop for them to review. In JavaScript, this can be easier than in most other languages due to the nature of it being run in a browser, readily available to be modified and prototyped with; an advantage Java Enterprise Applications can only dream of. We can work closely with the user experience designer adjusting the expected interface and at the same time change the workflow dynamically to suit our business needs, first on the frontend in the browser and later moving the knowledge out of the prototype to the backend, if necessary.

Managing an orc dungeon

When talking about domain-driven design, it is often stated in the context of having complex business logic to deal with. In fact, most software development practices are not really useful when dealing with a very small, cut-out problem. Like with every tool, you need to be clear when it is the right time to use it. So, what does really fall in to the realm of complex business logic? It means that the software has to describe a real-world scenario, which normally involves human thinking and interaction.

Writing software that deals with decisions, which 90 per cent of the time go a certain way and ten per cent of the time it's some other way, is notoriously hard, especially when explaining it to people not familiar with software. These kind of decisions are the core of many business problems, but even though this is an interesting problem to solve, following how the next accounting software is developed does not make an interesting read. With this in mind, I would like to introduce you to the problem we are trying to solve, that is, managing a dungeon.

An orc

Inside the dungeon

Running an orc dungeon seems pretty simple from the outside, but managing it without getting killed is actually rather complicated. For this reason, we are contacted by an orc master who struggles with keeping his dungeon running smoothly. When we arrive at the dungeon, he explains to us how it actually works and what factors come into play.

Even **greenfield** projects often have some status quo that work. This is important to keep in mind since it means that we don't have to come up with the feature set, but match the feature set of the current reality.

Many outside factors play a role and the dungeon is not as independent at it would like to be. After all, it is part of the orc kingdom, and the king demands that his dungeons make him money. However, money is just part of the deal. How does it actually make money? The prisoners need to mine gold and to do that there needs to be a certain amount of prisoners in the dungeon that need to be kept. The way an orc kingdom is run also results in the constant arrival of new prisoners, new captures from war, those who couldn't afford their taxes, and so on. There always needs to be room for new prisoners. The good thing is that every dungeon is interconnected, and to achieve its goals it can rely on others by requesting a prisoner transfer to either fill up free cells or get rid of overflowing prisoners in its cells. These options allow the dungeon masters to keep a close watch on prisoners being kept and the amount of cell space available. Sending off prisoners into other dungeons as needed and requesting new ones from other dungeons, in case there is too much free cell space available, keeps the mining workforce at an optimal level for maximizing the profit, while at the same time being ready to accommodate the eventual arrival of a high value inmate sent directly to the dungeon. So far, the explanation is sound, but let's dig a little deeper and see what is going on.

Managing incoming prisoners

Prisoners can arrive for a couple of reasons, such as if a dungeon is overflowing and decides to transfer some of its inmates to a dungeon with free cells and, unless they flee on the way, they will eventually arrive at our dungeon sooner or later. Another source of prisoners is the ever expanding orc kingdom itself. The orcs will constantly enslave new folk and telling our king, *"Sorry we don't have room"*, is not a valid option, it might actually result in us being one of the new prisoners. Looking at this, our dungeon will fill up eventually, but we need to make sure this doesn't happen.

The way to handle this is by transferring inmates early enough to make room. This is obviously going to be the most complicated thing; we need to weigh several factors to decide when and how many prisoners to transfer. The reason we can't simply solve this via thresholds is that looking at the dungeon structure, this is not the only way we can *lose* inmates. After all, people are not always happy with being gold mining slaves and may decide the risk of dying in a prison is as high as dying while fleeing. Therefore, they decide to do so.

The same is true while prisoners are on the move between different dungeons as well, and not unlikely. So even though we have a hard limit of physical cells, we need to deal with the soft number of incoming and outgoing prisoners. This is a classical problem in business software. Matching these numbers against each other and optimizing for a certain outcome is basically what computer data analysis is all about.

The current state of the art

With all this in mind, it becomes clear that the orc master's current system of keeping track via a badly written note on a napkin is not perfect. In fact, it almost got him killed multiple times already. To give you an example of what can happen, he tells the story of how one time the king captured four clan leaders and wanted to make them miners just to humiliate them. However, when arriving at the dungeon, he realized that there was no room and had to travel to the next dungeon to drop them off, all while having them laugh at him because he obviously didn't know how to run a kingdom. This was due to our orc master having forgotten about the arrival of eight transfers just the day before. Another time, the orc master was not able to deliver any gold when the king's sheriff arrived because he didn't know he only had one-third of his required prisoners to actually mine anything. This time it was due to having multiple people count the inmates, and instead of recoding them cell-by-cell, they actually tried to do it in their head. While being orc, this is a setup for failure. All this comes down to bad organization, and having your *system* to manage dungeon inmates drawn on the back of a napkin certainly qualifies as such.

Digital dungeon management

Guided by the recent failures, the orc master has finally realized it is time to move to modern times, and he wants to revolutionize the way to manage his dungeon by making everything digital. He strives to have a system that basically takes the busywork out of managing by automatically calculating the necessary transfers according to the current amount of cells filled. He would like to just sit back, relax and let the computer do all the work for him.

 A common pattern when talking with a business expert about software is that they are not aware of what can be done. Always remember that we, as developers, are the software experts and therefore are the only ones who are able to manage these expectations.

It is time now for us to think about what we need to know about the details and how to deal with the different scenarios. The orc master is not really familiar with the concepts of software development, so we need to make sure we talk in a language he can follow and understand, while making sure we get all the answers we need. We are hired for our expertise in software development, so we need to make sure to manage the expectations as well as the feature set and development flow. The development itself is of course going to be an iterative process, since we can't expect to get a list of everything needed right in one go. It also means that we will need to keep possible changes in mind. This is an essential part of structuring complex business software.

Developing software containing more complex business logic is prone to changing rapidly as the business is adapting itself and the users leverage the functionality the software provides. Therefore, it is essential to keep a common language between the people who understand the business and the developers who understand the software.

 Incorporate the business terms wherever possible, it will ease communication between the business domain experts and you as a developer and therefore prevent misunderstandings early on.

Specification

To create a good understanding of what a piece of software needs to do, at least to be useful in the best way, is to get an understanding of what the future users were doing before your software existed. Therefore, we sit down with the orc master as he is managing his incoming and outgoing prisoners, and let him walk us through what he is doing on a day-to-day basis.

The dungeon is comprised of 100 cells that are either occupied by a prisoner or empty at the moment. When managing these cells, we can identify distinct tasks by watching the orc do his job. Drawing out what we see, we can roughly sketch it like this:

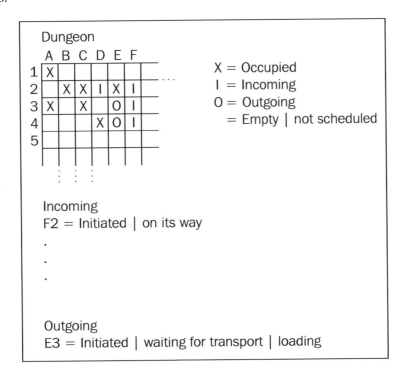

There are a couple of organizational important events and states to be tracked, they are:

1. Currently available or empty cells
2. Outgoing transfer states
3. Incoming transfer states

Each transfer can be in multiple states that the master has to know about to make further decisions on what to do next. Keeping a view of the world like this is not easy especially accounting for the amount of concurrent updates happening. Tracking the state of everything results in further tasks for our master to do:

1. Update the tracking
2. Start outgoing transfers when too many cells are occupied
3. Respond to incoming transfers by starting to track them
4. Ask for incoming transfers if the occupied cells are to low

So, what does each of them involve?

Tracking available cells

The current state of the dungeon is reflected by the state of its cells, so the first task is to get this knowledge. In its basic form, this is easily achievable by simply counting every occupied and every empty cell, writing down what the values are. Right now, our orc master tours the dungeon in the morning, noting each free cell assuming that the other one must be occupied. To make sure he does not get into trouble, he no longer trusts his subordinates to do that! The problem being that there only is one central sheet to keep track of everything, so his keepers may overwrite each other's information accidently if there is more than one person counting and writing down cells. Also, this is a good start and is sufficient as it is right now, although it misses some information that would be interesting to have, for example, the amount of inmates fleeing the dungeon and an understanding of the expected free cells based on this rate. For us, this means that we need to be able track this information inside the application, since ultimately we want to project the expected amount of free cells so that we can effectively create recommendations or warnings based on the dungeon state.

Starting outgoing transfers

The second part is to actually handle getting rid of prisoners in case the dungeon fills up. In this concrete case, this means that if the number of free cells drops beneath 10, it is time to move prisoners out, since there may be new prisoners coming at any time. This strategy works pretty reliably since, from experience, it has been established that there are hardly any larger transports, so the recommendation is to stick with it in the beginning. However, we can already see some optimizations which currently are too complex.

 Drawing from the experience of the business is important, as it is possible to encode such knowledge and reduces mistakes, but be mindful since encoding detailed experience is probably one of the most complex things to do.

In the future, we want to optimize this based on the rate of inmates fleeing the dungeon, new prisoners arriving due to being captured, as well as the projection of new arrivals from transfers. All this is impossible right now, since it will just overwhelm the current tracking system, but it actually comes down to capturing as much data as possible and analyzing it, which is something modern computer systems are good at. After all, it could save the orc master's head!

Tracking the state of incoming transfers

On some days, a raven will arrive bringing news that some prisoners have been sent on their way to be transferred to our dungeon. There really is nothing we can do about it, but the protocol is to send the raven out five days prior to the prisoners actually arriving to give the dungeon a chance to prepare. Should prisoners flee along the way, another raven will be sent informing the dungeon of this embarrassing situation. These messages have to be sifted through every day, to make sure there actually is room available for those arriving. This is a big part of projecting the amount of filled cells, and also the most variable part, we get told. It is important to note that every message should only be processed once, but it can arrive at any time during the day. Right now, they are all dealt with by one orc, who throws them out immediately after noting what the content results in. One problem with the current system is that since other dungeons are managed the same way ours is currently, they react with quick and large transfers when they get in trouble, which makes this quite unpredictable.

Initiating incoming transfers

Besides keeping the prisoners where they belong, mining gold is the second major goal of the dungeon. To do this, there needs to be a certain amount of prisoners available to man the machines, otherwise production will essentially halt. This means that whenever too many cells become abandoned it is time to fill them, so the orc master sends a raven to request new prisoners in. This again takes five days and, unless they flee along the way, works reliably. In the past, it still has been a major problem for the dungeon due to the long delay. If the filled cells drop below 50, the dungeon will no longer produce any gold and not making money is a reason to replace the current dungeon master. If all the orc master does is react to the situation, it means that there will probably be about five days in which no gold will be mined. This is one of the major pain points in the current system because projecting the amount of filled cells five days out seems rather impossible, so all the orcs can do right now is react.

All in all, this gives us a rough idea what the dungeon master is looking for and which tasks need to be accomplished to replace the current system. Of course, this does not have to happen in one go, but can be done gradually so everybody adjusts. Right now, it is time for us to identify where to start.

From greenfield to application

We are JavaScript developers, so it seems obvious for us to build a web application to implement this. As the problem is described, it is clear that starting out simply and growing the application as we further analyze the situation is clearly the way to go. Right now, we don't really have a clear understanding how some parts should be handled since the business process has not evolved to this level, yet. Also, it is possible that new features will arise or things start being handled differently as our software begins to get used. The steps described leave room for optimization based on collected data, so we first need the data to see how predictions can work. This means that we need to start by tracking as many events as possible in the dungeon. Running down the list, the first step is always to get a view of which state we are in, this means tracking the available cells and providing an interface for this. To start out, this can be done via a counter, but this can't be our final solution. So, we then need to grow toward tracking events and summing those to be able to make predictions for the future.

The first route and model

Of course there are many other ways to get started, but what it boils down to in most cases is that it is time now to choose the base to build on. By this I mean deciding on a framework or set of libraries to build upon. This happens alongside the decision on what database is used to back our application and many other small decisions, which are influenced by influenced by those decisions around framework and libraries. A clear understanding on how the frontend should be built is important as well, since building a single-page application, which implements a large amount of logic in the frontend and is backed by an API layer that differs a lot from an application, which implements most logic on the server side.

 Don't worry if you are unfamiliar with express or any other technology used in the following. You don't need to understand every single detail, but you will get the idea of how developing an application with a framework is achieved.

Since we don't have a clear understanding, yet, which way the application will ultimately take, we try to push as many decisions as possible out, but decide on the stuff we immediately need. As we are developing in JavaScript, the application is going to be developed in Node.js and express is going to be our framework of choice. To make our life easier, we first decide that we are going to implement the frontend in plain HTML using EJS embedded JavaScript templates, since it will keep the logic in one place. This seems sensible since spreading the logic of a complex application across multiple layers will complicate things even further. Also, getting rid of the eventual errors during transport will ease our way toward a solid application in the beginning. We can push the decision about the database out and work with simple objects stored in RAM for our first prototype; this is, of course, no long-term solution, but we can at least validate some structure before we need to decide on another major piece of software, which brings along a lot of expectations as well. With all this in mind, we setup the application.

In the following section and throughout the book, we are using Node.js to build a small backend. At the time of the writing, the currently active version was Node.js 0.10.33. Node.js can be obtained from `http://nodejs.org/` and is available for Windows, Mac OS X, and Linux. The foundation for our web application is provided by express, available via the **Node Package Manager** (**NPM**) at the time of writing in version 3.0.3:

```
$ npm install -g express
$ express --ejs inmatr
```

For the sake of brevity, the glue code in the following is omitted, but like all other code presented in the book, the code is available on the GitHub repository `https://github.com/sideshowcoder/ddd-js-sample-code`.

Creating the model

The most basic parts of the application are set up now. We can move on to creating our dungeon model in `models/dungeon.js` and add the following code to it to keep a model and its loading and saving logic:

```
var Dungeon = function(cells) {
  this.cells = cells
  this.bookedCells = 0
}
```

Downloading the example code

You can download the example code files for all Packt books you have purchased from your account at `http://www.packtpub.com`. If you purchased this book elsewhere, you can visit `http://www.packtpub.com/support` and register to have the files e-mailed directly to you.

Keeping in mind that this will eventually be stored in a database, we also need to be able to find a dungeon in some way, so the find method seems reasonable. This method should already adhere to the Node.js callback style to make our lives easier when switching to a real database. Even though we pushed this decision out, the assumption is clear since, even if we decide against a database, the dungeon reference will be stored and requested from outside the process in the future. The following shows an example with the find method:

```
var dungeons = {}
Dungeon.find = function(id, callback) {
  if(!dungeons[id]) {
    dungeons[id] = new Dungeon(100)
  }
  callback(null, dungeons[id])
}
```

The first route and loading the dungeon

Now that we have this in place, we can move on to actually react to requests. In express defining, the needed routes do this. Since we need to make sure we have our current dungeon available, we also use middleware to load it when a request comes in.

Using the methods we just created, we can add a middleware to the express stack to load the dungeon whenever a request comes in.

A middleware is a piece of code, which gets executed whenever a request reaches its level of the stack, for example, the router used to dispatch requests to defined functions is implemented as a middleware, as is logging and so on. This is a common pattern for many other kinds of interactions as well, such as user login. Our dungeon loading middleware looks like this, assuming for now we only manage one dungeon we can create it by adding a file in `middleware/load_context.js` with the following code:

```
function(req, res, next) {
  req.context = req.context || {}
  Dungeon.find('main', function(err, dungeon) {
    req.context.dungeon = dungeon
    next()
  })
}
```

Displaying the page

With this, we are now able to simply display information about the dungeon and track any changes made to it inside the request. Creating a view to render the state, as well as a form to modify it, are the essential parts of our GUI. Since we decided to implement the logic server-side, they are rather barebones. Creating a view under `views/index.ejs` allows us to render everything to the browser via express later. The following example is the HTML code for the frontend:

```
<h1>Inmatr</h1>
<p>You currently have <%= dungeon.free %> of
<%= dungeon.cells %> cells available.</p>

<form action="/cells/book" method="post">
  <select name="cells">
    <% for(var i = 1; i < 11; i++) { %>
    <option value="<%= i %>"><%= i %></option>
  <% } %>
  </select>
  <button type="submit" name="book" value="book">
  Book cells</button>
  <button type="submit" name="free" value="free">
  Free cells</button>
</form>
```

Gluing the application together via express

Now that we are almost done, we have a display for the state, a model to track what is changing, and a middleware to load this model as needed. Now, to glue it all together we will use express to register our routes and call the necessary functions. We mainly need two routes: one to display the page and one to accept and process the form input. Displaying the page is done when a user hits the index page, so we need to bind to the root path. Accepting the form input is already declared in the form itself as /cells/ book. We can just create a route for it. In express, we define routes in relation to the main app object and according to the HTTP verbs as follows:

```
app.get('/', routes.index)
app.post('/cells/book', routes.cells.book)
```

Adding this to the main app.js file allows express to wire things up, the routes itself are implemented as follows in the routes/index.js file:

```
var routes = {
  index: function(req, res){
    res.render('index', req.context)
  },

cells: {
  book: function(req, res){
    var dungeon = req.context.dungeon
    var cells = parseInt(req.body.cells)
    if (req.body.book) {
    dungeon.book(cells)
  } else {
    dungeon.unbook(cells)
  }

    res.redirect('/')
  }
 }
}
```

With this done, we have a working application to track free and used cells.

The following shows the frontend output for the tracking system:

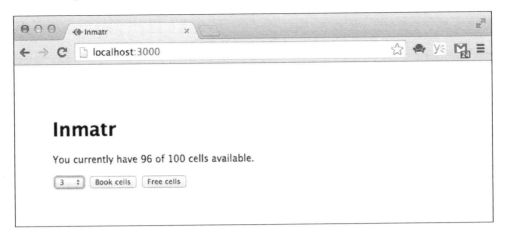

Moving the application forward

This is only the first step toward the application that will hopefully automate what is currently done by hand. With the first start in place, it is now time to make sure we can move the application along. We have to think about what this application is supposed to do and identify the next steps. After presenting the current state back to the business the next request is most likely to be to integrate some kind of login, since it will not be possible to modify the state of the dungeon unless you are authorized to do it. Since this is a web application, most people are familiar with them having a login. This moves us into a complicated space in which we need to start specifying the roles in the application along with their access patterns; so it is not clear if this is the way to go.

Another route to take is starting to move the application towards tracking events instead of pure numbers of the free cells. From a developer's point of view, this is probably the most interesting route but the immediate business value might be hard to justify, since without the login it seems unusable. We need to create an endpoint to record events such as fleeing prisoner, and then modify the state of the dungeon according to those tracked events. This is based on the assumption that the highest value for the application will lie in the prediction of the prisoner movement. When we want to track free cells in such a way, we will need to modify the way our first version of the application works. The logic on what events need to be created will have to move somewhere, most logically the frontend, and the dungeon will no longer be the single source of truth for the dungeon state. Rather, it will be an aggregator for the state, which is modified by the generation of events.

Thinking about the application in such a way makes some things clear. We are not completely sure what the value proposition of the application ultimately will be. This leads us down a dangerous path since the design decisions that we make now will impact how we build new features inside the application. This is also a problem in case our assumption about the main value proposition turns out to be wrong. In this case, we may have built quite a complex event tracking system which does not really solve the problem but complicates things. Every state modification needs to be transformed into a series of events where a simple state update on an object may have been enough. Not only does this design not solve the real problem, explaining it to the orc master is also tough. There are certain abstractions missing, and the communication is not following a pattern established as the business language. We need an alternative approach to keep the business more involved. Also, we need to keep development simple using abstraction on the business logic and not on the technologies, which are provided by the frameworks that are used.

Another look at the problem

So far, we have been looking at the application solely from a web developer's point of view. This is a classic case of *when all you have is a hammer, everything looks like a nail*. Have we really tackled the core problem already? What questions haven't we asked yet? These are important things to ask ourselves. Also, we need to figure out what we can ask our business experts to get a better idea on how to move forward. So what assumptions did we make beforehand and why?

Using the right tool for the job does extend to the abstractions that we make. Solving a problem when you already know the *solution* is a web application, which is not always helpful.

Thinking in an MVC web application

So far, we have been thinking about the problem in terms of a **Model-View-Controller** (**MVC**), web application. This brings along a certain set of assumptions that might not hold true in the case of our business domain. It is true that creating a web interface to manage input and output often does handle the presentation of an application today, but this does not mean that this part also holds the primary set of logic. In the case of our dungeon manager, it might only be one way to access and input data. An information system structured in this way has models holding the logic along with the data. These models are backed by a database, which is responsible for persistence, and is also used to implement some logic via constraints on the data. This means that our domain is pressed in the shape of the, most likely relational, database model.

All this locks us into a certain set of technologies: a webserver for hosting our application, a database for persistence, and a web layer for access and input. All these elements become the integral parts of our application and make change hard. Also, the model layer has no real abstraction besides being composed of a bunch of models. When we want to represent more complex interactions, this might not be enough. To be clear, there is no real issue with this as long as the developed application primarily consists of the interaction between systems, when however, the value proposition is mainly the business logic to be represented between parts of the system, this design starts to be not enough anymore.

Understanding the core problem

In the case of business applications, a lot of problems and their respective solutions are often not explicit. This is true for many areas and an example most developers might be familiar with is setting up a webserver. When asking a developer or administrator what he has to do to achieve this, it is described in only a few steps along the lines of: set up the operating system, install **Apache**, configure the site, and then start. For another developer of a system administrator, this might be enough to know what to do, but this is hardly reproducible for somebody from the outside or, even worse, for a computer.

Making all the steps explicit is essential to get a grasp of what the core business domain really consists of. In our case, we need to make sure to follow what the orc master currently does to keep his dungeon running. This can be done by either following him around, or making him walk us through his normal business process. We can't, however, rely on the business expert to explain the process to us in the necessary details. Also,we can't rely on our understanding of it to match what really needs to be done.

The main goal of this exercise, therefore, is to establish a baseline of understanding for what is going on and provide a shared language to talk about the problems, which will inadvertently arise. We are in an uncertain situation to start out with. This should not scare us, but we need to see it as the opportunity to increase our own understanding, as well as sometimes even the understanding of the currently executing person. Often business experts realize new details about their domain when questioning all the steps towards a goal, and they might even identify the possible problems.

 Figuring out where the gaps in understanding a business process are is half the battle to implementing it correctly.

In the case of implementing a business process, we can assume that the status quo is the least we need to replicate to replace the tools the business is currently using. So, first of all, we need to either rebuild or incorporate all the tools the business is currently using. We can later find the places where optimization makes sense and is possible when we get a firm grasp on the problem in general. We should also aim for gradual replacement of processes one by one instead of one big switch, as this minimizes the risk for the business.

Communication is key

There are only two hard things in Computer Science: cache invalidation and naming things.

Phil Karlton

When working with applications, it often is a problem to create a shared language between developers, product owners, as well as the business people in general. It is often stated that naming things is one of the hardest problems of computer science, and it is true that having a describing name makes many things easier. It is also often the case that a clearly named object is easier to extend because its scope is already defined by its name. Therefore, it is often discouraged in object-oriented design to name things with general words, such as *Manager, Creator* or *Processor*. When thinking about this problem in the context of our business domain, it becomes clear that we can, and should, reuse the established business language as often as possible. It all comes down to communication. We, as the developers, are new to the field, so the business experts introducing us will already have an established language to describe problems in the domain where we are missing them.

As we follow along the steps of our business expert, we should take the time to get accustomed to the specific language that is in use throughout. This becomes even more essential as we start writing code. We will constantly need to check in with the domain experts to take their understanding into account, so when we use the business language to encode the domain, it will be easier for us to talk to everybody around us to develop a better understanding of the domain. This is quite abstract, so let me give you an example. Consider this naming for the dungeon:

```
function Dungeon(cells) {
  this.freeCells = cells
}
```

Now consider we want to record changes in the amount of prisoners, and write the following code:

```
var dungeon = new Dungeon(100)
dungeon.freeCells -= 5
dungeon.freeCells += 3
```

Even though this is natural to a developer, it does not use any business-specific language. We need to explain the meaning of things like += to non-developers to make them understand the meaning. Consider on the other hand encoding the same logic in the following methods:

```
Dungeon.prototype.inPrison = function (number) {
   this.freeCells -= number
}

Dungeon.prototype.free = function (number) {
   this.freeCells += number
}
```

Using these methods to express the same thing, it looks vastly more domain - specific then before. We can now describe the problem in the context of the domain and the code looks as follows:

```
var dungeon = new Dungeon(100)
dungeon.inPrison(5)
dungeon.free(3)
```

It will now become quite clear, even to non-developers, what is going on and therefore we can focus on talking about if the behavior is correct rather than about the details of the code.

The concepts of domain-driven design

When developing software, it is all too easy to get caught up in the details of implementation, without ever getting to the bottom of the problem. As software developers, our main goal is always to add value to the business, and for this to work, we first need to be clear what the problem we are trying to solve is. This has been attacked in several ways throughout the history of computer science. Structured programming gave the developers a way to break a problem into pieces, object-orientation attached those pieces to named things that allow for further structure and better associate meaning with parts of the program.

Domain-driven designs focus on getting structure in the problem solving process and also provide the right starting point to begin a conversation every stakeholder can be part of. Language is an important part in this, since communication is an area where a lot of projects struggle, as there often is a mismatch between engineering and business. While engineering terms are often more specific, the business language leaves room for interpretation, leaving it up to the person and his or her context to resolve what has been talked about. Both forms of languages have their place, as they have been established as an effective form of communication in their specific scenario, but translating between these two is often where problems or bugs are introduced. To help with these problems, domain-driven design allows a developer to classify certain types of object in the communication in several forms, all of which are going to be introduced in detail throughout this book:

- Value objects
- Entities
- Aggregates
- Bounded context

These are concepts that have a certain meaning and allow classification objects, which are part of a business process. With this, we can attach meanings and patterns.

It is all about distractions

Considering the different ways to create a program, the main improvement that structured programming added to the way we program today is the idea that while working on a project, the programmer does not always have to have the whole project in his head to make sure to not duplicate functionality or interfere with the regular flow of the program. This is accomplished by encapsulating functionality in chunks to be reusable in other parts. Moving onward, object-oriented programming added the ability to further encapsulate functionality in objects, keeping data and functions together as one logical unit. One can say a similar thing for functional programming, which allows the programmer to think about his program as a flow of functions that are defined by their input and therefore can be composed as larger units. Domain-driven design now adds a layer on top, which adds abstractions to express business logic and can encapsulate it from the outside interaction. Creating a business layer that interacts with the outside world via a clearly defined API does this in this case.

Looking at these different practices, one thing shines through on all levels, and this is the idea of removing distractions. When working on a large codebase or on a complex problem, the more you have to keep in your head at once, the higher the level of distraction from the core problem. This is a major point of **domain-driven design**, and we are going to see how this plays out in the next chapter when we think about how we can go from a specification that we have seen before, toward a problem description we can continue to work with.

Focus on the problem at hand

In a lot of cases, stating the problem is actually not obvious. This is why working towards a shared understanding between business experts and developers is so important, both sides need to agree on what they expect from a feature, or a piece of software. Allowing developers to state in clear terms to the business what the feature solves allows the developers to focus on the problem at hand and get input more directly. Similar to the principles of test-driven or behavior-driven development, stating in a clear fashion what something is intended to do helps the development a long way. At this stage, creating a route to get from *A* to be *B* as well as objectively stating when a goal has been reached, is what we seek. This by no means saves us from reconfirming that the goal is still the one to achieve constantly with the business, but it allows us to make this communication clear. With the language established, this now does not have to involve multiple hour-long meetings with no clear outcome.

With all this in mind, it is now time to dive into the essence of domain-driven design. Throughout this book, we are going to move our orc dungeon to the 21st century, allowing it to flexibly adjust to its business needs. As a first step, we are going to sit down and see what running this dungeon is all about and how our new software can add value using the concepts and the mindset of domain-driven design.

Further reading

Domain-driven design, as seen in this chapter, is described in large by the book *Domain-driven design*, by Eric J. Evans. I would recommend every reader to follow up with his descriptions to provider a deeper insight into the ideas behind domain-driven design in general, outside a more specific topic as described here.

Summary

In this chapter, we went through the steps of getting started with an application as most projects are started today and contrasted it with the domain-driven design approach to development. We learned about the key focus of domain-driven design, as the communication between the developers and the other parties involved in a project.

The key point to takeaway is the strong focus on getting the core feature set of the application, before focusing on technology choices and other development-related problems that will otherwise subtract resources from the exploration. Another important aspect we learned about is how to gather specification in terms of usage. The key point here is to gain knowledge about how the work is currently achieved and how the application can help besides asking potential users for a specification.

The next chapter focuses deeper on the process of gathering knowledge about the use, expected usability of the application, and on the process of starting to build a language to aid the communication between the team developing the application, build domain experts and developers.

2

Finding the Core Problem

Every piece of software is written to solve a problem, and in turn is a perfectly valid solution for this exact problem. Sadly, the problem a piece of software solves so perfectly is not always the problem the software was created for in the first place or even the problem the programmer had in mind when the software was written. The history of programming is full of examples where developers tried various ways to come up with a way to be able to perfectly state a problem first, and then implement a solution. Developing software based on the waterfall model is a great example of having a nice idea that failed to deliver on the promise. When you ask the parties involved about the failure, the reason will most likely be that the problem diverged from the specification, or the specification was misunderstood in—according to one party—a very obvious way. So, why is this?

When starting a software project, especially one motivated by a business need, we set out to model a part of the real world and apply a set of constraints and algorithms to it, to ease the job of one or more parties involved in the business. The problem is that the party that has the issue the developer is trying to solve is most likely not the developer. This means that the developer first has to get an understanding of what the request really is to actually know what is supposed to be developed.

How can we get a deep enough understanding of a certain part of the business without the (most likely) years of experience our clients have ahead of us? The solution to this, and the most likely problem, is communication. We need to find a way to explore the problem deeply enough, and backed with our knowledge of how to model a world in software, to be able to ask the right questions. We need to do this in such a way we don't lose the non-technical people so that we can draw from their understanding. This comes back to the language mismatch between developers and business people, and it is probably the biggest obstacle to overcome. In domain-driven design, this is referred to as the **ubiquitous language** of the project, a language shared by all parties involved in the project. Establishing this kind of language allow us to communicated clearly across team boundaries, and as mentioned before, this is one of the core ideas in domain-driven design.

Coming back to our example of the orcs running a dungeon, we don't know how this is done; we don't even completely understand the constraints that cultural aspects involve or apply. The world of the orcs is one in which we are an outsider who can only watch, ask questions, and model it according to our understanding. We naturally have to trust the local experts. Even though we aren't as much of an outsider in real-world problems, we should always try to view the problem from the outside as much as possible because, in a business that has taken years to grow, our own assumptions are probably wrong anyway.

In the following, we are going to explore the problem and introduce a set of tools that will help to do this. We will cover several aspects, but most importantly the following:

- Using pen and paper for programming
- Code spikes and throwaway code
- Mapping our actors out—creating a dependency graph for our domain

Exploring a problem

There are not many problems in software development that can be fully specified easily. Even the few that seem like it leave some room for interpretation. When working on a project to implement a database adapter, I recently faced exactly this. There was a specification that needed to be implemented, and a set of unit tests making sure the implementation conforms to the specification. However, as I implemented it, I found myself asking questions along the way. The main question was very similar to what I would have asked if I hadn't had the specification: How are people going to use this piece of code? In a lot of cases, there are multiple ways to implement a certain feature, but picking one often means weighing different tradeoffs against each other, such as speed, extensibility, and readability.

In our orc dungeon, we have to ask the same basic question: How is the client going to use our software? Sadly, this question by itself will not yield the results we have in mind. The problem is that our users don't know our software. Basically, our future users have the same problem we do: they don't know what the software is going to look like when it is finished but can only guess its usage. This really is the *catch 22* of software development; thus, so to be successful, we need to find a way around this. We as developers need to find a way to make the process of development possible to grasp for our future users, and our future users need to adapt concepts of the highly descriptive language we use to state intentions as clearly as possible.

Software is really an abstract concept, and most people are not used to talking about abstract things. So, the first step toward a better understanding is to make it more approachable for the users. We need to make the concepts *touchable*; this can be done in various ways, but the more haptic the better.

> Use paper. As developers, we often prefer to go paperless, but writing things on paper makes it easier for most people to understand concepts, so writing things down can be immensely helpful.

Outlining the problem

As far as techniques to illustrate and organize pieces of information go, *outlining* proves useful in many cases. But, how can we outline software? The idea is to keep all the information that comes up when talking to the business experts in an easily searchable format. In a lot of places, this is a *wiki*, but it can also just be a set of shared text files that are readily accessible whenever information needs to be added or retrieved. Outlining here means to store information nested by topic and drill down as needed.

Tracking knowledge

When starting with collecting information, the most important part is to collect as much information as possible, and to do this it needs to be made seamless. It is also important to keep the information organized to be added to as well as to be restructured as needed. As with our software, we don't know the structure of the outline to start out with, so we just add a new piece whenever we identify a new entity, actor, or any important piece of the system. Therefore, don't invest too much time making the current structure perfect, but rather make it just good enough for now.

> Make a habit of collecting any information that you come across, and keep the application outline at hand. In a lot of companies, the hallway track is often an immensely valuable source of information, so make sure to use it.

What makes an outline so useful is that you will be able to restructure it easily, and this is also what you should aim for when deciding on the tool to keep these outlined notes. Reordering notes needs to be quick and intuitive. The goal right now is to keep the cost of change as low as possible, so we can easily explore different paths.

Our dungeon information that we collected so far can be represented like this:

```
# Dungeon
receives prisoners
transfers from other dungeons
new captures
loses prisoners
transfers to other dungeons
fleeing
prisoners might flee during transfer
prisoners might flee from the dungeon itself
```

The important part is that this structure is very easy to modify and keep up-to-date as new information arrives, and we can already see that a new entity emerges from the outline—the prisoner. With this new information, we now add this to the outline to have a place to hold more information about prisoners, since they are obviously a vital concept to our dungeon application.

```
# Prisoner
can flee a dungeon or transport
needs a cell
is transferred between dungeon
```

This is essentially what the outline is about, recording information and drawing quick conclusions.

The medium

Depending on the situation, different mediums are possible or preferable to hold the information. This can stretch from a piece of paper up to a full-blown wiki system. The format I prefer to use for my outlines is **Markdown**, which has the advantage of being stored as plain text and being very readable without being processed. Also, to generate some documentation to print out, it is useful to process it to HTML first. This is by no means the ultimate choice, and you should choose whatever feels the most natural, as long as it is simple to edit and readily available in as many places as possible. The one thing that is important, is to choose a system that does not lock you in to its way of doing things or as into a data format that is hard to export or change.

Paper programming

In our quest to involve non-programmers in the process of software creations, it is important to make concepts approachable. We need to illustrate interactions as well as actors of the system and make them ready to be moved around. Often, it helps to have something people can actually hold in their hand and move across a table when talking about a subject. The best way to achieve this is to create paper representations of the elements of the system. Create a paper-based, hand-operated version to touch and interact with right there and then. This is often known from UI design, where paper prototypes are a common thing, but it also works well to create a version of non-UI parts of the application.

The idea is to draw out any pieces of the system on cards to be combined, separated, and added to. When this is done, it often ends up being pretty close to the entity representation we will later have in the system. When starting out using this technique, it is important to note that the end result will always be in a certain state. As things get moved across the table, and elements are modified, we need to keep track of the information that is generated. Make sure to keep notes along the lines of how certain actions evolved during the discussion as a single picture of the end result is just reflecting one state.

So how does such a paper program work?

When starting out, we lay out all the information we currently have, drawing out boxes for all the elements, and name them. In our case, we will draw out the dungeon, prisoners, cells, and a transport. For now, these are the entities we interact with. At this point, we think about a specific interaction and try to represent it with the entities and other objects we currently have. Let's transfer a prisoner from our dungeon into another; to do this, we need to think what we have to do:

- The dungeon keeper notifies the other dungeon
- The prisoner is transferred from a cell onto the transport
- An orc is assigned to guard the transport
- The transport travels to the other dungeon

When drawn it out on a sheet of paper, the result may look a little like this, where the numbers are the order in which the steps appeared:

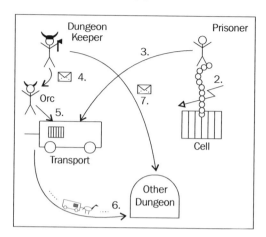

At this point, we already notice that multiple pieces are missing, mainly the dungeon keeper and some way to notify the other dungeon. So, how can these be added? The dungeon keeper clearly is an entity that manages the dungeon, so a separate card should be added. Also, the notification is done via messages, so we add a messaging system. This is a new subsystem, but we can for now consider it a black box we can drop messages into have them arrive at the other side.

Now that the systems are in place, we can add the needed methods to the actors of our system: The dungeon keeper, to request a transfer, needs a way to send a message; the cell needs to give up the *ownership* of the prisoner; the transport needs to take ownership; and so on. As we move through this interaction we can clearly see one possible way this can be modeled and this is also more approachable for non-developers as they see actual boxes moving across the table. As this model is in constant flux, make sure to keep notes in your outline along the way, to not lose any of the newly acquired information.

Not so scary UML

Our paper, a prototype, gives us a nice picture of the interaction, and our outline captures a lot of information about how the program should behave in various cases. It also captures details on the naming side of things from a business perspective. All in all, this gives us a lot of good insight, but there is still a part missing. This makes the information out of our paper prototype durable enough, so we can more easily reference it as we move along. The prototype we drew earlier is missing some information that is important to the implementation. We need to capture more of the structure of the application.

This is the point where **Unified Modelling Language (UML)** comes into play, yes this scary piece of waterfall-infused practice that most of us never thought of as being useful. When talking about UML is it often referenced as the idea to encode all modeling information in a diagram; so ultimately code could be generated and filled out by basically everybody with some amount of coding skills. Of course, this does not work, but UML still has some interesting properties that make it useful. What we are setting out to do is leveraging one property of UML, and this is the ability to capture interactions in a concise form. UML defines multiple categories of diagrams:

- Structure diagrams
- Behavior diagrams
- Interaction diagrams

A **structure diagram** focuses mostly on the actors in the system and their relationships. In our case, it would express the relationship of the keeper toward the dungeon and other orcs for example. This can be helpful when many actors are involved, but is not necessarily the most important information to start out with.

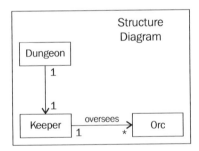

A use case diagram gives a slightly more detailed picture of the actors in the system, and their interaction with each other. A use case diagram is part of the behavior diagram family and therefore focuses on the behaviors of the actors. This is not only useful information for our system, but also too coarse grained at the moment to express the flow of information and actions.

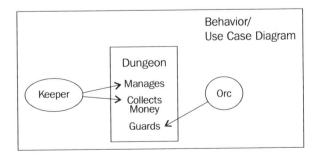

As our feature does involve interaction between the defined actors of our system, a useful thing to explore is the sequence of events as they happen in our system. For this, we can use a sequence diagram, which is a type of interaction diagram in UML. This kind of diagram focuses on the sequence of events that need to happen to achieve a certain goal. Some of this may be asynchronous, some needs to await a response; all this is captured in a single diagram:

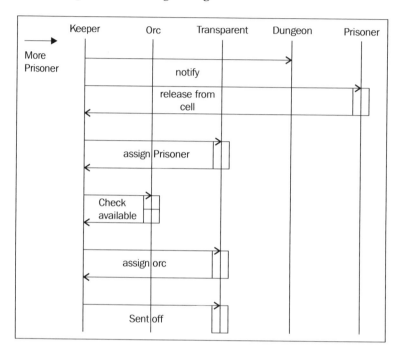

With this kind of illustration, it is easy to distinguish between synchronous and asynchronous messaging, so we can be sure to model the methods accordingly. Also, naming things is known as one of the hardest problems of computer science, so be sure to show this to your domain experts to draw from their language to name the now exposed messages and methods.

So far, the idea of every part has been to have the tools to explore the problem from different view perspectives, but don't drink too much of the Kool-Aid! We don't try to create a complete description of the whole system, but rather explore one part just deeply enough so that we can get a sense of what its core functionality is going to be and how it makes sense to implement it. We can then remove the uncertainties, by asking the right questions as we know the domain well enough so that we are able to explore the business domain together with the experts.

Involving the experts

As we explore the domain from every angle, it is important to talk to the people who know as much as one can about it. One of the core ideas of domain-driven design is to create a language around the domain that can be spoken by each party involved. When talking about the tools, we set out to create them in such a way developers as well as domain experts can take part on an equal footing, so each can draw from the other's knowledge to approach a problem.

The spoken language is a problem in itself, so for developers it needs to be as unambiguous as possible, because very concrete and specific ideas need to be expressed. There should be no room for misinterpretation. For business people, on the other hand, it needs to be understandable for such a non-technical audience. Now comes the important part, where we actually are going to see whether we have achieved this goal so far, and how we are able to communicate the ideas of the domain back and forth.

When involving the experts of a domain, we should first have a clear idea of what we are trying to achieve, such as gaining knowledge about the system we are currently developing. It is a natural tendency for developers to make their system shine in the best light, but our goal is to expose misunderstandings and uncertainties in our design and understanding so far. We actually want to get caught *off-guard*, so to speak. For the current stage of the project, this should be considered an achievement. Right now, change is as cheap as it is going to get, so if we expose a certain gap in our knowledge, we make our lives easier down the road. Getting a misunderstanding exposed right now also means that we were able to ask all the right questions such that we were able to communicate this abstract idea of a software system successfully; thus, the business side was able to dive into our system and correct the flaws. If we get to this point, non-developers are actually involved in the development and we can move forward developing a very well-suited system. So, how do we get there?

Finding the gaps

The first thing we now have to do is to start the conversation flowing. As with most problems, it is best to think about them in a diverse group, so we get the most viewpoints. To get there, we want to create an environment where the business domain experts can explain to us what is going on. We can use all the different techniques now to talk about our software in an accessible fashion. The idea of paper programming can come in very handy at this stage.

So first we need to prepare, make sure all the units that have been identified are prepared. Have cards ready for everybody to move around and write on them as the actions are illustrated and gaps are identified in the knowledge. It is also helpful to take a picture of the current state with notes attached to save the state for later reference as the ideas evolve. The conversation can start out with the developers explaining how they think the system works, encouraging the business experts to interject whenever there is something unclear or just plain wrong. This can really become a kind of game. How can an action we want to express be expressed with the pieces available? Of course, this is not a puzzle, so you are able to create new pieces at will and change them as needed. Being guided through the process in such a way will most likely expose several valuable properties in the system.

[Being precise is what it is all about; make sure to ask questions such as *And this is how it is done 100% of the time?* as often as possible.]

So, let's walk through an example feature of our software: transferring a prisoner to another dungeon.

Talking business

The process of transferring a prisoner has been described in three steps:

1. The dungeon keeper notifies the other dungeon.
2. The prisoner is transferred from a cell onto the transport.
3. The transport travels to the other dungeon.

So, we have some cards prepared:

- The notification service identified by an envelope
- The dungeon cell
- The prisoner
- The transport

With the available cards, we can let the orc master describe precisely what needs to happen when a prisoner is transferred.

The orc master identifies the problem, as follows, and sends out a raven with the notification of the transfer request to the dungeon. He then goes to the cell to move the prisoner out and on to the transport, assigning an orc to guard the transport and sending it off to the other dungeon.

In this short description, we see multiple differences from our model that need to be addressed.

1. The order of one and two does not actually matter, as long as there is at least one prisoner in the dungeon, which we can check at notification time.

2. There is going to be another scarce resource involved, and these are the guards to man the transport; they need to be available, and their flow in and out will need to be tracked.

Given the new insights, we can now model this event as actors in our system pretty accurately. It is important to note that our system of course does not need to represent the flow directly in code but, from a high-level point of view, having a consistent flow makes sense since it has established itself through (possibly) years of practical use. Thus, it is at least a good point to start after all.

Talking about the actors

When talking about how to implement a certain feature, several forms of objects are involved, all of which have certain distinct roles in the system. A lot of these roles exist in many systems, even though they may be named differently. In a domain-driven design, the classification of these roles makes a big difference. The reason is that, if we classify something, there is a certain set of patterns that can be applied right away, since it has proven itself to be useful. This is very similar to the idea of naming the patterns that have emerged in enterprise applications and are by now almost basic knowledge to most application developers.

In domain-driven design, we have multiple building blocks to choose from:

- Entity
- Value object
- Aggregate
- Domain event
- Service
- Repository
- Factory

Most of the elements in this list probably make sense to you as a developer already but, if not, we are going to define each of these more explicitly later. For now, let's focus on the ones we need and we are already using in the system: aggregate, value-object, and domain events.

One important distinction is the difference between an entity and a value object. While an entity is defined by its identity, a value object is defined by its properties. Going back to our prisoners and cells, we can see that it is possible to use either classification, but it changes the focus. If a prisoner is an entity, each prisoner is clearly defined, and two prisoners will always be different. Classifying them like this makes prisoners traceable throughout the system, as they move from dungeon to dungeon and cell to cell. This may be really useful, but may be an overkill as well. This is what the current stage is all about—finding the focus of the project from a domain point of view. So let's walk through the whole process step by step.

Starting from the outside in, we first have to think about our domain event. As the name suggests, this is the event that triggers a certain reaction by the domain; in our case, this is the transfer of prisoners. To handle the events, we have to move one level down and think about the parts of our system that handle the transactions on our resources, the aggregates. They are, so to speak, the actors in the system as they aggregate all the needed entities, value objects, and everything else needed to present a consistent view to the outside world. Aggregates are also responsible for changing the state of the world in our system according to the domain's need. As far as aggregates go, there are multiple ones that are responsible for the action: the dungeon keeper managing cells, prisoners, and keepers, as well as the transport being a mobile cell, the prisoner, and the keeper. Notifications to other dungeon live somewhat outside the system, so classifying these as a service seems like the natural thing to do. OK, this wasn't too hard, and thinking about the classification of different object is quite natural.

Using the provided domain terms lets us state the intended focus and level of the parts clearly. Other developers, even if they are unfamiliar with the system, are now able to assume a given feature set from each named entity. For us, the naming is a form of documentation that allows us to notice quickly when we start to intermix concepts.

Identifying the hard problem

Over the last sections, we started to gain a solid understanding of the interactions in the system. Now it is time to leverage this understanding and move on to implementing our software solution. So, what should we start with when developing the software?

Often when a project is started, we like to start with the easy part, maybe create a project from a template—for example, running a framework code generator, such as Node.js Express, in a new folder to set us up with the scaffold structure for our project. At first, this seems like a really good option as it creates a lot of the boilerplate code we would have to write to create an Express project otherwise. But, does it move use closer to solving a business problem? We now have a code base to explore but, as it is auto-generated, we don't have any domain-specific code obviously. On the other hand, we have locked ourselves in a fixed structure. For some projects, this is a good thing; it means that there are fewer things to think about. However, if we try to solve a lower-level problem, it is arguably bad to lock yourself into a certain mindset.

We need to identify the problem and determine how to deliver value to the business as fast as possible. This will drive user adoption and development of the software further. So far, we explored one part of the domain, which seemed important enough to our business to explore implementing it as our first feature. Now, it is time to drill down into it to see where the core problem lies, seeing the objects that will be involved and their interaction with our software.

Mapping the dependencies

From our previous work, we have a pretty clear understanding of the objects involved, at least on a high level:

- Notification Service
- Cell
- Prisoner
- Keeper
- Orc master
- Transport

With these in mind, our task is now to find a place to start. When laying out these objects, it is clear that they all have some dependency on other parts, and we can leverage this. We draw up each object, using arrows to demonstrate which objects it depends on. This is known as a **dependency graph**:

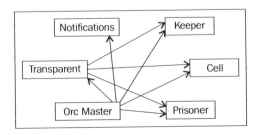

The graph shows us the dependencies for each of the actors we identified. The keeper, for example, is a necessary dependency for the transport as well as the orc master. On the other hand, the orc master depends not only on the keeper, but also on the transport, prisoner, and cell as well. Looking at the graph, we can see in which order the elements need to be implemented. Elements we identified as aggregates before are of course going to have the most dependencies. They, as their name suggest, aggregate multiple objects into one unit for common access and modification.

One way to attack the problem is to start out in the following order:

1. Keeper.
2. Cell.
3. Prisoner.
4. Transport.
5. Notification service.
6. Orc Master.

The nice thing is that, along the way, we can present an intermediate state back as soon as one of the aggregates is in working order. We can talk about our idea of a transport, and align it with the expected feature for example. The working condition is an important point here, since it is really hard for people to judge a certain piece if it does not satisfy the requirements in multiple ways. Of course, "working condition" does not mean that we actually see something but, as the software gets more complex, we are able to use those aggregates to play the role in the operations they are designed for. We may, for example, create a quick prototype that replays some interactions specified by the business team. This of course goes hand in hand with testing and feature acceptance tests or behavior-driven development.

 Presenting an intermediate state to the domain experts needs to involve guidance on the feature, as well as asking questions along the way. Throwing partially implemented software *over the fence* is hardly of any use.

Drawing with code – spiking

After we now have an idea where to start developing, we can finally explore how to actually do it. When we think about the problem, we may have some idea how it works, but there are also going to be pieces where, though we know how the high level operates, we are unclear about the lower levels. When a developer does not know how something will work in reality, the best way to figure out what to do is by actually trying it and exploring the libraries and tools that are deemed useful along the way.

This approach is referred to as **spiking**. We create a throwaway code, which is just there to explore a certain difficult part, without the intention of having this code ever make it into production. This frees us from a lot of the intricacies that are often involved in creating production-ready code. The code is there just to solve a specific case and help us gain knowledge about how to solve the same problem later. Most developers know that the first approach is hardly ever the perfect solution to a problem, so let's just deal with this fact by creating a first version that we intend to throw away. A spike is all about the knowledge gain and not about the code, so be ready to write something quick and dirty just to make it work. This can actually be a really fun exercise, by the way!

A common area to spike is the interaction with external services, such as our notification service where the interface is known on a high level but the developer has actually never worked with it. Since we don't have any idea how to interface with a Raven, I'm going to leave this for now. We will need to revisit this when the situation comes up but, as we learned from our UML diagram, the process is asynchronous anyway. Therefore, we don't expect that a response can hide behind a *Mock* in our first prototype.

The other interesting problem is going to be creating the interface between our code and the users. We can't be sure how the users want to interact with the software, since there is no experience in using anything like it. Interfaces tend to give us more insight into what the users want out of the software as well. The way a user wants to use a software teaches a lot about his focus and expected features, so spiking it is a great way to learn more about the system. This spike can be done in multiple ways, but it is actually useful to have real interface elements to build on and that can later be filled with more interactions. One way of doing this is to create the interface in HTML, which provides the basic structure but without the interactivity and fill in the gaps with JavaScript as we move along. For the sake of brevity, the code is omitted. If you are interested, visit the code repository for the book and check it out.

Keep in mind that this is not actually an interface we intend to keep, but we can now show something to our users and explain how they will interact.

Getting started, it's about time

With the previous work done, we are now at a point where we can start to work on the first feature of the application. We explored our ideas as far as we needed, and are in a position where we can actually talk about the details with our domain experts. I simplified the steps to get here a bit in the sense that we only talked about one iteration. In reality, this process most likely takes several iterations where your own understanding of the problem evolves. Sometimes not only your understanding changes, but often the business side also refines its own understanding along the way as well.

Creating value without creating code

As programmers, we often feel that the value we create is tied to the code we create, but this is not true, I will even go as far as to say that our value lies in the code we don't create. The simpler we can make a problem, the easier it is to move the project forward, and simplicity is based on a solid understanding of working together with the business as a team.

[There is nothing easier to create than complexity, so watch out! Solving a problem in the simplest way possible is what every piece of software should aim to do.]

When we walk through the process as we have done earlier and let people explain what they do each day, it is not rare to discover how something can be simplified and improved. It is part of the software development process to try to improve the process itself as well. As we explore the idea behind a feature, and let the business side talk about its own actions, it is common that they themselves notice unnecessary overhead or even process inherit complications that don't need to exist. This is the reason why we try to explore in the way we have done earlier in a textual format. Don't begrudge the time it takes to explore, but keep in mind that right now you are already creating value for the business, and an improvement at this stage is a great success.

Deciding on the first feature

Even though we have already been moving the business forward, it is now time to actually do what developers do best—write code. The exploration we performed now points us towards starting out with the following feature set.

We want to automate the process of moving prisoners out of our dungeon and keep a record of the prisoners moved at the same time. This seems really valuable, since an overflowing dungeon is a major problem for the orc master. This is also a part of the larger problem of keeping a record of the prisoners inside the dungeon and that we saw as part of our outline. Ultimately, this is what we set out to do. After this first feature is done, the moving of prisoners will be almost completely automated and will therefore save time we can invest into other elements of running the dungeon.

We flushed out a basic interface to handle this, and it seems to be great to work with. So, let's start coding and set up a project using the techniques of domain-driven design to move the project along.

Summary

In this chapter, we learned how we can get started with a project prior to writing code. We focused on the interaction with the business experts, providing them with feedback by illustrating our thinking. We covered the importance of gathering knowledge and how to organize that knowledge so we can leverage it later on in the project to understand the goals of the application we are building.

As we moved forward, we looked into how to identify the core feature set and choose a good starting point to not only provide value to the business early on, but also to help us further understand the business domain. This process is similar to the goals of agile methodologies, trying to cover the core problems early on and provide quick value and feedback to the business.

In the next chapter, we are going to get started setting up the project and covering the important details to get a good grip on managing the process throughout development.

3
Setting Up a Project for Domain-driven Design

So far we have been focused on getting the prerequisites for the project ready. We focused on creating a mental model for ourselves and confirmed that our understanding of the domain matched the understanding of our domain expert. By doing this, we started to create a shared language between all the people involved so that all parties can communicate about the project while avoiding most misunderstandings. With all this in place, we were able to identify a starting point for the project, and now that we know where to start and how to name our objects according to the domain, we can set up the project to fit this. Robert C. Martin says in his talk *Architecture the lost years*: *Architecture is about intent* that architecture is not created for the sake of itself but actually to state what the project is about and make it clear for the next person what each level covers. As we set up our application, we want to express what the application is about at every level, and this includes the level of organization of files and folders as much as it is about creating classes and modules.

Our main goal, which coincides with the goal of software architecture, in general has been to not make decisions prematurely as well as to ensure the decisions we make are as self-explanatory as possible. We have not decided on any frameworks or actually any technology yet, but as we now push our application forward, it is time to resolve some of those deferred decisions, even though we want to keep as much as possible open to change.

This chapter is going to be about the challenges that arise when it comes to creating a flexible project setup that allows your project to adapt and actually embrace a change of structure. This is important to keep in mind throughout the whole design as we put it together. We don't want a module structure hindering our refactoring, or making our project more rigid because of an overwhelming class and file hierarchy.

As we go about this, we are going to deal with structure on multiple levels:

- File and directory structure
- Project structure
- Object or class structure
- Application structure as interaction with the outside of the domain

Object and class structure, as well as project structure, are closely related to how we decide to design our application. As part of this, testing is introduced as it has the most immediate impact on how we are going to design both our classes and objects. It also has an impact on the way our team works together on the project and how they are able to show the results to business experts by letting them explore the project as it currently stands.

 As JavaScript leaves the realm of enhancing websites and moves towards being a language used for large applications, be it in the browser or on the server, the need for more involved architectures has grown and people have tried to carry over many of the concepts currently in use for Java or C++ backend applications. Often this actually causes more problems than it solves, as JavaScript is a very flexible language and has its own concepts of how organization can, and should, be done even though parts might still be missing; modules being one of those as a core concept. When building a JavaScript application, always keep in mind what language you are using and use its features and concepts to work with your project; don't fight it every step of the way.

This chapter covers the setup of the project and how to make it a joy to work on. You will learn about the following:

- The project file structure and what to consider when laying it out
- Different forms of testing and why they are important
- Building the application
- An introduction to hexagonal architecture

Structuring a project as we see it

As a new developer dives into a project, the first thing they are always going to see is the layout of files and folders in the project. This is also the element of organization we deal with constantly while editing the project, so it is worth investing thought into the organization. Just looking at the files and folders should already tell you something about the project; it is the highest level of organization and therefore should represent some of the top level concepts of our domain.

So to start out, we need to make sure we know what we are trying to solve with this structure. There are multiple points that we need to address at this level, and they will follow us through every part of the organization of the project; they are:

- Approachability
- Locality of edits
- Fitness for handling change

So let's see what these points are about and how we can optimize for each of those points.

Approachability

As a new developer joins a project, or even as one comes back to a project that they have not been recently working on, there is a learning curve in knowing where things are located, and maybe even more importantly in where things should be located moving forward. This is always a problem as it slows down development, or when talking about an open source project it might actually slow down adoption and contributions. So we obviously want to make codebase as approachable as possible, but what does this mean? There is a subjective learning curve in relation to unfamiliar tools and styles, which is hard to estimate ahead of time for each developer, but there is also a more objective one in relation to common practices, naming, and well established concepts. So how can we make a codebase approachable just from the file and folder level?

When we start out, we will need to take a look at what is in there, so the ease of navigation is one of the first things we have to deal with. Having extensive levels of subfolders, with only view files, or sometimes even no files, is an example of making a project hard to navigate. Some might say that the editor you are working with should solve this, but it is also a problem we create for ourselves, so we should refrain from it.

There are more ways to make a project approachable so, for example, the filenames should reflect the contents, as should the directory names, and probably most importantly, the project should follow conventions that have been established in the community. This means that unless you have a very good reason, you should refrain from creating your own conventions. Especially little things such as naming files according to a community standard can help a lot. One example is tagging on names like model or controller to the end of files. In some programming communities this is really common, while in the Node.js community it is frowned upon. Following these little things can make it easier for developers as not following them might almost drive rage towards a project.

Keep in mind that files will most likely only ever be touched by developers, so they can be optimized to support developers in their task, and so a common developer practice is of higher weight than approachability for a domain expert. Of course, the extent of this varies between projects and tasks. It holds largely true for the organizational nature and for common idioms from frameworks, but does not extend to the naming of the inherent part of the language that is developed throughout the project. We want the project's structure to be approachable for developers already familiar with similar codebases, but we don't want to introduce a translation layer between the developers and the domain experts.

Let's take a closer look at this in an example of how we could lay out the basics for our dungeon-manager. To start out, this will, of course, only contain the transferring `prisoners feature`, but nonetheless it will hint towards the overall structure:

```
├── index.js
├── lib
│   └── prisoner_transfer
│       └── index.js
├── package.json
└── test
    └── features
        └── prisoner_transfer_test.js
```

The important thing to note about this structure is that it uses the basics of node modules all the way while already hinting at a possible structure to include multiple features outside the prisoner transfer. The `index.js` files are conventional named to indicate the entry point to a certain module. A developer jumping into the project will know to look in those files first when trying to find out more about the module. We can leverage this fact later to include common documentation about the feature, as well as having this file load all the others necessary to accomplish the module task.

Creating the tests in a test folder is also the established way to locate your tests. As the test have certain categories inherent in their design, it makes sense to structure the test directory accordingly. The structure of the test folder should allow us to, at a glance, figure out what tests there are and how they apply to our project as a whole. As the project grows, having a set of tests covering the features is not only incredibly valuable from a regression perspective, but also gives a quick insight into how a certain feature can be used, so locating your tests quickly can mean a certain module gets reused or adapted instead of wasting efforts on duplicating what was there already.

 The structure presented here is not set in stone, some people prefer app to lib, spec to test, or other small changes like this. The goal of a structure should always be that developers feel at home in it. Tradeoffs in this area can be made with specific developers in mind.

Lastly, adding a `package.json` file is the common way to handle project dependency and to define aspects about the structure and other parts, so we add this as well, ready to put to good use later.

Locality of edits

As developers are working on the project, they are most likely working on either a feature, or are fixing bugs and refactoring code. As these activities are, at least in the case we are aiming for, related to one feature, we want to make sure that the developer does not have to jump into many different places to edit. The files related to the problem should therefore be in one spot, reducing the overhead of opening everything related to a given task or feature, as well as the mental overhead of keeping the related parts in one's head to make sure the edits happen in the right place.

This is one of the reasons we created features such as packages or modules in the `lib` folder before. As the developer works on the prisoner transfer, they can, just by looking at the directory structure, know what to edit. They can quickly open the files in their editor and view them as a unit of work as they are changing the code to accomplish a given task.

Using a structure like this not only makes it easier to look at for the developer when editing, but also the version control system will be easier to work with. As the code is organized like this, we can look at it on a feature-by-feature basis and we are also less likely to touch the same files when working on different features. This not only reduces the likelihood of conflict, but also makes the history of a given module more useful.

If you look at the preceding structure we have been using so far, you might have noticed that the locality of edits breaks down for tests. As we work on the prisoner transfer feature in `lib`, we have to edit the feature test in tests as well, which is about as far apart as you can get filesystem-wise. As with everything in software development, this is a tradeoff and we have chosen approachability over locality in this case. The reason being that a higher value is placed on the onboarding of people, and the assumed cost of non-locality seems low enough to support that. If we think otherwise, we might locate the tests for each feature inside the feature, and therefore more easily enable moving the whole feature to a different project in the future. This decision is not all or nothing of course, and we might create a structure resembling the main structure under the test directory to keep a locality for the tests as part of the tests directory for example.

Fitness

Fitness, according to Darwin, means the capacity to survive and reproduce.

Darwinian fitness - Lloyd Demetriusa, Martin Ziehec

As our software grows and evolves, it will need to adapt to varying scenarios of its usage, and the best software is the kind that grows beyond its intended use case. A common example is Unix and the associated philosophy. The idea is to create many small pieces that, when recombined, allow for a vast variety of uses. Unix has survived in various forms for decades now and there does not seem to be an end in sight, but being created in a certain way is only half the story. As changes came along and new use cases took form, it did not ossify, but its idea and concepts were malleable, but what does that mean for our software. How can we achieve similar versatility?

We have seen already that even on the filesystem level, the software is composed of modules. There is an obvious distinction between the different elements as features are implemented. From a fitness perspective, this means that we are quickly able to locate a certain feature, as well as enhance, remove, or reuse it. A feature should also hint at its dependencies, which could be made clear through subfolders, or just by looking at the imported dependencies located in the index file located right at the root of a feature directory.

To give an example, moving forward as the dungeon manager grows, the prisoner transfer might start to incorporate more messaging since other dungeons have adopted our system, and we can now fully automate transfers between them. At this point, the whole kingdom relies on the availability of the transfer service and this means that very rigorous testing needs to be present to ensure its reliability because downtime means that the kingdom cannot raid at maximum effectiveness. We are very happy with the success of this system, but it slows down development of the dungeon manager in general, as the prisoner transfer is a part of it and we need to comply with its harsh integration rules. But we are in a good position after all; if we look at the layout of our application, we can see that we can quite easily extract the prisoner transfer into an application by itself and have it maintained separately.

After the extraction, we can start moving forward quickly again, and integrate the transfer as just another service the dungeon manager speaks with. Splitting out common functionality, as well as functionality that has to comply with different constraints, is key to having malleable and extendable software that can keep moving forward.

In reality, this would obviously be the best case, but just structuring an application as a set of independent small parts all tested separately on the feature level makes us consider APIs in a way that will be very useful down the road as the software grows and, of course, the same goes the other way around. We are able to rip out unneeded features quickly and thus reduce the maintenance overhead and increase our velocity. This is in essence the concept of cooperation of all the small Unix programs mentioned at the beginning of this section.

This is not the *be all and end all* of software design of course, as anybody who started out using Unix mainly from the shell will know that the initial learning curve is rather steep and getting anything done does not feel very fast or expressive at the beginning. As we have seen before, reaching all the way for one goal means sacrificing another, in this example—the approachability of the project. After all, there is no perfect solution, but at least at the beginning of a project it is often helpful to enhance approachability and think about other problems as they arise. For us, this means that keeping a high level structure of modules in mind is probably a good thing, but going overboard and making every piece ready for extraction, or even its own application, will probably not help the project along.

Don't overcomplicate things to get the perfect architecture, as it does not exist. It is more important to get the software into the hands of the users quickly to get feedback on whether it is even useful. A slowdown determining the perfect architecture will most likely be more costly down the road due to the delay in feedback, than a suboptimal architecture could be.

Dealing with shared functionality

As we have structured our application right now, we are ready to split apart features that might become an independent piece of functionality, but what about the other way around? Domains often have a certain set of key concepts that to shows up time and time again. This is great as it allows us to not having to write it over and over if we can share it across the pieces that need. It also shows that we understand the domain well enough to extract core concepts and share them, so it is actually something to strive for.

This is great on a level where our features match the shared functionality closely; we provide a public interface and each dependent interface can develop against that. But what happens if we actually extract a piece of functionality, and our prisoner transfer service is for example no longer local to the application but actually a service that is reachable via HTTP for example? In this case, we have to deal with shared functionality, which is not just another thing we can create an API for, but we actually have to implement the same code in every dependent to actually call over the API to do the work we were doing locally before. Think of the payment gateway abstraction every other shopping system creates—this kind of functionality could be developed once and used in multiple places, allowing shared testing and shared resources for development.

This is, of course, not the only place where shared functionality actually means there is code being shared, where it seems like we have to duplicate certain snippets all over the place. Other examples might be database access, or configuration management. What all of this has in common is that it is actually lower level code that does not really have a close relationship with the application domain. We are dealing with an artifact of the way we like to communicate, and the patterns we applied don't support this communication well. We can think about it also in the way that the cohesion at a domain level is low, because we are leaking abstractions in a way that would for example make us care about the database accessing code when we want to deal with a prisoner.

 One thing to keep in mind when introducing shared code is that sharing is coupling and coupling is not a good thing. There should always be a very good reason for sharing code.

Multiple solutions are possible at this point, and depending on the project as well as the piece of code, different ones might be applicable, so let me introduce you to the most common ones.

A shared toolbox

When the first shared functionality appears that does not really belong anywhere, most projects start to create a *utility* library, a toolbox of things that are used in places all over the project. Even though many architecture purists frown upon it, it might be the best way to start out. It is better to have a shared toolbox separated out than dealing with code duplication later on after all. Many popular libraries start this way; think about underscore providing its implementation of the *each* construct on top of JavaScript, and dealing with all the different versions underneath that a browser implementation might have to care about to run all over the world. The following is an example from the `underscore.js` file, reformatted for easier reading:

```javascript
var each = _.each = _.forEach = function(obj, iterator, context) {
  if (obj == null) return;
  if (nativeForEach && obj.forEach === nativeForEach) {
    obj.forEach(iterator, context);
  } else if (obj.length === +obj.length) {
    for (var i = 0, length = obj.length; i < length; i++) {
      if (iterator.call(context, obj[i], i, obj) === breaker)
      return;
    }
  } else {
    var keys = _.keys(obj);
    for (var i = 0, length = keys.length; i < length; i++) {
      if (iterator.call(context, obj[keys[i]], keys[i], obj) ===
      breaker)
      return;
    }
  }
};
```

While a library such as underscore is a perfect example of the usefulness of this approach, there are problems as well. Especially when poorly named, this folder or file quickly becomes the dumping ground for all kind of things. It is quicker to not think about where something really belongs, and instead just dump more into the utilities folder. At least it is in one place now where it can be moved and refactored from, so stay positive; it could be worse. In the long run, the goal should be to move to an approach where we use object orientation and let our tests guide a domain-design from the start. When we look at an application and we see a library function like the above being part of the application code we know that there is an abstraction missing. Again, it is all tradeoffs all the time and the problem with abstractions is that you have to consider them at the time of writing.

Utilities or libraries are a dangerous place, so be sure to keep them on your regular review and refactor radar. Always leave the code a little bit tidier than you found it and monitor its churn closely.

Moving up the dependencies

As the project moves along and grows, the best way to deal with dependencies will probably be to leverage what is there already. Your libraries have grown, and many internal projects rely on them, so why not make use of the dependency management that is built into the environment already?

JavaScript used to be notoriously bad at dealing with dependencies, but the time of downloading a version of jQuery and putting it in the project is luckily over. JavaScript provides an amazing amount of dependency managers for every use case. In the browser, we can leverage **bower** (`http://bower.io/`), **browserify** (`http://browserify.org/`) and **npm** (`https://www.npmjs.com/`) and possibly many more, and in Node.js, npm is the standard way to deal with any kind of packages we might want.

Depending on the kind of library that has been developed as part of the process, it might be either a good point to rely on versioning it outside of your project, or even maybe set up a private version of the package registry. This will be overkill in the beginning, but is something to keep in mind as the need arises. Also, don't forget that it might be your time to contribute back to the community and release it as open source.

Testing

Beware of bugs in the above code; I have only proved it correct, not tried it.

Donald Ervin Knuth

Every system that is supposed to go into production needs to be evaluated against the real world situation. Reality can be a harsh thing, and it happens more often than not that something we expected to work perfectly fine does not work when we actually want to use it. So throughout the history of computer programming, developers have thought about how they could make sure that the software works, and at best, actually work as expected.

In 1994, Kent Beck wrote the **SUnit** test framework for Smalltalk and kicked off the modern age of unit testing. The idea was quite simple: automate the evaluation of code and make sure it fulfilled a certain set of specifications. Even though there are many new frameworks today to achieve this, the basic idea is still the same: write code and check whether it produces the expected result. In reality, with or without a testing framework or fixed process, developers are always doing this—nobody is just pushing code into production without actually having tried it before, at least. We can either do this by hand, or automate it.

There are multiple points that need to be addressed to make testing useful because there are different goals for the tests we write. We need to facilitate easy unit testing, expressive feature testing, and performance testing. This of course does not mean that all scenarios need to be handled by one framework, but the less friction there is, the better the adoption of the core principles will be. It is also vital to make sure the tests are executed, and the best way to achieve this is through automation, making sure no code can wind up in the end product without satisfying its requirements and without breaking others.

Setting up a test environment

As we now know, there are a lot of different goals a test environment must satisfy, but there also are an incredible number of test frameworks out there and JavaScript itself brings some challenges when it comes to testing. One framework that has worked for a lot of projects in the past is the Mocha-testing framework. It has also gained quite a wide adoption among web developers, so the following sections will explain Mocha. There is no secret to it, and Mocha is swappable for the framework of your choice that fits the style of your development team best. The only thing to make sure is that you actually use what you have, and be aware of what you want to get out of your tests. So first, we need to make sure we know what the goals are for our different tests before we can chose a technology to achieve them.

Different types of tests and goals

When we start testing code, there are multiple reasons why we should do it. For a project that is driven by its domain implementation, one major aspect is always testing the features as they are implemented, as we want to provide quick feedback to the client and show in an explanatory way that our implementation works. But as developers, we also need to dig a little deeper and work on the unit level, exploring the specifics of our code as we write it, or as we design the algorithm. Finally, a project should not only care about its functionality in actually doing what it is supposed to do, but also be usable from a user perspective, giving responsive answers and performing well enough overall to not be in the way. All of these aspects can be achieved by testing.

Feature specs

Making tests not only useful for the developer, but for the client too, has been the ultimate goal of test driving and implementation for many years. There are tools such as **Ruby's Cucumber** that have a JavaScript implementation that makes sure the specification gets somewhat decoupled from the code, making it as accessible as possible for the domain expert to read and understand. The end result is a specification that mostly looks like plain English but has some restrictions applied to it. The code below is using the cucumber syntax to describe the prisoner transfer as a feature specification, including one acceptance scenario:

```
Feature: Prisoner transfer to other dungeon
  As a dungeon master
  I want to make prisoner transfer an automated process
  So no important steps get left out

  Scenario: Notifying other dungeons of the transfer
    Given I have a prisoner ready to transfer to another dungeon
    When I initiate the transfer
    Then the other dungeon should be notified
```

This kind of specification can now easily be turned into a running specification, using the `Given`, `When`, and `Then` blocks as the instructions for our tests.

Decoupling the specification from the real tests like this somewhat removes the programmer from it. So, depending on the technical expertise of the product owner, the idea is that even they could write the specification, with some developer support of course. In most projects, this is not the case, and the developers end up creating the specification code for Cucumber, as well as its implementation as test code. In this case, it is useful to stick with more basic tools, as it is a better fit for developers to write tests in a way they are accustomed to already. This does not mean Cucumber's idea isn't something to keep in mind. Tests should read at a really high level, and should be understandable to reflect what the product owner originally intended when describing it to developers, so we can detect mismatches together as a team. But, as code is most likely to be read with a developer at hand, the overhead of having almost two implementations of the tests is unnecessary.

There is nothing wrong with being inspired by Cucumber and using Mocha to write our tests. The tests can look like this for example:

```
var prisonerTransfer = require("../../lib/prisoner_transfer")
var assert = require("assert")

describe("Prisoner transfer to other dungeons", function () {
  /*
```

```
 * Prisoner transfers need to be an automated process. After
 * initiation the transfer should take the necessary steps to
 * complete, and prompt for any additional information if needed
 */

it("notifies other dungeons of the transfer", function (done) {
  var prionser = getPrisonerForTransfer()
  var dungeon = getDungenonToTransfer()
  prisonerTransfer(prionser, dungeon, function (err) {
    assert.ifError(err)
    assert.equal(dungeon.inbox.length, 1)
    done()
  })
})

// Helpers
/* get a prisoner to transfer */
function getPrisonerForTransfer() { return {} }

/* get a dungeon to transfer to */
function getDungenonToTransfer() { return { inbox: [] } }
})
```

Even though this style is now actual runnable code, using helper methods to abstract details and make the naming clear keeps it readable. The goal here is not to make it easy for a non-technical person to read this, but to enable a developer to sit down with a business expert and talk about the implied rules.

 Test are an integral part of the code, so they need to have the same rigorous coding standards employed, and since there are no tests for the tests, readability is key.

Unit tests

After the discussion with the business expert to agree on the feature set, and creating a specification of its current state in the feature specs, there is a level where we as developers need to try out our code. This is where unit tests shine! The idea is to test our code as we develop it and allow it to be immediately executed in isolation, where we can reason about it. Unit tests are generally quickly changing as the development on a certain part progresses and serves as regression protection afterwards.

Don't fear throwing away unit tests; they are there to aid development not to hinder it.

As we already are using Mocha for our features, it is natural to use it to test our smaller units as well, but the tests are going to look different. At the level of the unit tests, we want to isolate ourselves as far as possible and if we can't do that, then we are really going to encounter some pain sooner or later in other development areas as well. This pain is really about high coupling; when we are coupling a module too close to other pieces of the system the test will show us. In this kind of setup, creating a unit test that is isolated is going to require an incredible amount of setup to really make sure we only hit the module by itself, and don't touch the dependencies.

The end result of unit tests of a module should always test the public interface and this interface alone, because at this point they serve as regression protection. The more external pieces are tested with the unit tests, the more of its private interface is exposed, the more likely a breakage is going to occur, but even though this is our end goal, don't make the mistake of thinking this should be all the unit tests ever do. Often when writing a module of a bigger application, it can be immensely useful to explore its logic more deeply, especially when the public interface might still be in flux. So write all the tests that reach inside the harder parts of the module while developing it, but make sure you remove those "little helpers" before declaring a module ready for consumption.

Performance tests

Any time an application is moving forward and features are implemented, there is a point at which we need to think about the performance of this application. Even before we get into performance needs, it is important to know which parts of the system are most likely to cause trouble in the future.

The important thing about performance tests are that they will ascertain the focus on metrics in the code at an early stage. Just thinking about how to measure the performance across parts of the system will ensure that we think about instrumentation, and this can be a vital feature when we actually move closer to heavy usage later on or actually when exploring breakages in production.

Testing the performance of an application is, of course, not a one-off thing. By itself, a measurement of performance is rather meaningless; it only becomes useful if it's monitored as it changes over time. One strategy to accomplish this is exercising the outside API on each push to the master branch and recording the changes. This will give you an idea of where the project stands in respect to monitoring as well as performance over the time the project is developed.

Even though it might not be obvious outright, monitoring changes in performance is a major point towards implementing a domain. As developers employing domain-driven design practices, we must consider the usability of our app. Often, different stakeholders have different needs in performance, and having an application that does not satisfy its needs might render it useless to some. So many times apps stop being used due to bad performance characteristics even if they supply the whole feature set otherwise. Overall, just knowing the deficiencies is half the battle. When we at least have an understanding of where time is spent, it is a point where we can hook in as the need arises and optimize as needed. This need is very likely to arise sooner or later so the preparation for it is time very well spent.

With these different goals in mind, we now have to tackle the problem of actually running all those different tests as often as possible without having to rely on just strict compliance throughout, especially when creating a view over time. As a project changes, relying on people running everything needed every time is not just a major burden on the team, but unnecessary as well.

Continuous integration

In the end, all the tests one could ever want are only useful if they are run, and this is where continuous integration comes into play. Of course, all of us are great developers who always test their code, but even we might not always test the whole chain of integration in our app. Our performance tests are only useful if they are run on a comparable platform.

Continuous integration has been around for some time now, and its most prominent system is probably Jenkins, but others are around as well. The idea is to run the tests and other steps we need to move from development to production on a system automatically, and make sure we have a stable build at all times. We can even use this system to automate deployment, and of course provide a dashboard for developers to check how the app is doing right now.

A system like this can be a vital part of a project, as it allows you to quickly move from development to system, where the business experts can check the impact of the work as well. There are many tutorials out there on how to set up a project's continuous integration, and in recent times highly refined systems such as **Travis-CI** make it very easy to set up, so I won't go into more details here; just keep in mind that such a system is worth its cost many times over throughout a project that grows to a certain size and complexity, and there is no real reason not to use one.

A continuous integration system is really about keeping the best practices enforced throughout the development, even when a developer has a bad day. It also provides a more approachable way to have an outsider discover and evaluate the state of the application as a whole.

Managing the build

Writing software for an orc dungeon has a major advantage since the orcs don't know much about software so we can introduce any tools we like and they won't have an opinion on it. Why have I mentioned this when the title of this section is supposed to talk about building the software, you might wonder? There are a myriad of build tools out there and they all do things slightly differently, and everybody seems to prefer one to the other. Especially in JavaScript, the community has not yet standardized a tool so there is **Grunt**, **Jake**, and **Broccoli**, just to name a few, and of course your project might leverage one from a different language such as Ruby's Rake or the old familiar make.

Even though there are so many build tools, the only important thing about them is to actually use one. Yes they all have differences, but they can all do pretty much the same, adjusting for syntax and performance. But why is a build tool so important? And why should we use one?

Why every application needs a build system

Creating software at the scale of actually creating a functional, complete system to manage a business process is always a difficult task. Such a system involves many parts, like in our example of managing prisoner transfers, notifying other dungeons, tracking statistics about the dungeon, and so on. When we set it up, we need to load multiple files, maybe compile some parts, manage the dependencies, and, in the case of frontend JavaScript code, we also want to compress and minimize it to optimize for faster page load. Doing all this manually involves multiple steps and will most likely fail sooner or later because we forgot one of those steps, and this is where the build system comes in. In a way, all software has a build system, it just depends on how automated the system is.

 A build system optimizes for *boringness*; the more boring a build is, the better.

The goal is to not be able to make mistakes and create a reproducible environment every time. We want to run one command and get the expected result, so in our case the build system has a couple of responsibilities:

- Running the tests
- Packaging the application
- Deploying the application

All those steps are important to think about, so let's walk through them.

Running the tests

We are writing great tests right now and those tests ensure that our system behaves as expected according to the feature set we worked out with the domain experts, so those tests should run, and if they fail there is something wrong with our system that we need to fix. Since we already have a testing framework in place, running the tests is pretty straightforward:

```
$ mocha --recursive test
```

This will run all the tests specified inside the test directory, which according to our file layout we created earlier, will be all of them. Since we don't want to remember this command, we can wire it into npm by adding it to the package.json file we already set up:

```
{
  "name": "dungeon_manager",
  ...
  "scripts": {
    "test": "./node_modules/.bin/mocha --recursive test"
  }
  ...
}
```

With this in place, running all our tests becomes:

```
$ npm test
```

This will make our lives a lot easier, we can now rely on one command to actually run our tests, and the failures are certainly development failures and not the mistyping of a command, for example, forgetting about the --recursive and then skipping most of the tests. Depending on the preference of the developers involved, we can go even further, watching the files for changes and rerunning the tests triggered by those changes, the described system here should be considered as the minimum requirement.

Packaging the application

Moving an application to production is most likely not a one-step process. Web applications might involve compiling assets together, downloading dependencies, and maybe even configuring certain parts for production instead of development. Running these steps by hand is prone to error, and every developer who has used such a process before has a story to tell about it failing more or less spectacularly. But if we want to keep our software malleable and able to react to changes to the domain, as well as get it in the hands of our domain experts quickly, we need to deploy early and often, and the first step towards this is packaging the application in one step.

The goal is for every developer to be able to set up the basic environment for the application, like in our case installing Node.js, and from then on setting-up the application with one command. Continuing with npm for now to manage our task, we add the following to our `package.json` file:

```
{
  "name": "dungeon_manager",
  ...
  "scripts": {
    "test": "./node_modules/.bin/mocha --recursive test",
    "package": "npm install && npm test"
  }
  ...
}
```

Since this is a custom command that has no special support in npm running, it means running:

```
$ npm run package
```

This is a little non-intuitive to an outsider, but listing a command like this in the readme file will cover that for now, and if we want to, we can also decide on a system to wrap all those calls to make them consistent.

Now that we have a place to put any steps involved in packaging the application, we are ready to make sure we can deploy it with one command as well.

Deploying

Like we said before, we want our deployment to be a boring process; it should be one step and never cause a failure that is hard to recover from. This actually means we need to be able to roll back deploys as necessary, otherwise the fear of making a wrong deploy will be ossifying to any progress.

The actual deployment can be quite simple, and a couple of shell scripts easily accomplish it depending on your needs. One system that covers the basics, and is easy to use and adaptable to changing needs is `deploy.sh` is available at `https://github.com/visionmedia/deploy`. When using deploy, all there is to do is create a `deploy.conf` configuration file:

```
[appserver]
user deploy
host appserver-1.dungeon-1.orc
repo ssh://deploy@githost.dungeon-1.orc/dungeon_manager
path /home/deploy/dungeon_manager
ref origin/master
post-deploy npm run package && npm start
```

The file can be extended for any application servers, and should be fairly easy to read. Any steps that need to be run can be implemented as pre- or post-deploy hooks, which makes this system incredibly flexible, especially when combined with a powerful build system managing the application parts.

Choosing the right system

So far we have been using what was available without really installing big tools; `deploy.sh` itself is just a shell script containing less than 400 lines of code and npm comes with Node.js by default. There are a lot of valid reasons to actually use a system outside the ones that come with the environment, for example, when you expect that the project will be composed of more than one language in the future, choosing a neutral wrapper can greatly increase the consistency across projects and ease the on ramp.

We now know what we want to get out of the system, so choosing one means looking at the requirements and picking one the majority of the developers like. One thing to bear in mind is that this is something the project will stick with hopefully for a long time, so a system that has some usage under its belt is a good idea.

 I like to wrap most of my projects in a simple **Makefile**, because it is the most available and understood system out there, but your mileage may vary.

This brings us to the end of the setting up where we think about files and running commands, but one important part is missing, that is, how to actually make the domain part of the world, but keep it separate enough to allow reasoning on about it.

Isolating the domain

Create your application to work without either a UI or a database so you can run automated regression-tests against the application, work when the database becomes unavailable, and link applications together without any user involvement.

Alistair Cockburn

When we create an application following the principles of domain-driven design, we strive to keep the business logic separate from the parts of the software that interact with the "real world". The most-often referenced case is that we don't want to build our UI layer in a way that it houses some or all of the business logic as well. We want a clear domain-focused API that is consumed by other parts of the application to provide their interaction with the domain.

The concept is similar to the UI being provided by some, to the UI specific language or API, be it HTML, or for example QT. Both sprang out of the concept of providing the developer with all the parts needed to build a UI but keep a natural separation. This doesn't make sense, the combination of HTML, CSS, and the DOM abstraction of JavaScript are a DSL, domain-specific language, to build browser interfaces. They provide an abstraction under which the browser implementers are free to change their implementation without impacting every website written. They therefore isolate the business domain of the browser vendors, displaying structured content, from the job of creating the content, most likely your job. Having such an API has many advantages over exposing the internal data structures directly, as history has shown.

The architecture of modern applications

The idea to isolate the business domain has followed the software industry for a long time, especially with the growth of having a core domain and many consumers. In recent years, the idea to make a service an API first has become more and more viable due to the increasing importance of mobiles and the web. Many applications today have multiple interfaces, for example, in hotel booking, the state of the hotel is accessed by the employees, moving customers between rooms, taking bookings over the phone, and more. At the same time, customers are online, checking the Internet for available options and booking via various web portals.

On the days prior to their arrival, users might want to access the data on their phone in a mobile app to make sure they have it available wherever they are. These are just some of the many access options for a booking system, and even now there are a lot of options already:

- Internal desktop applications
- Internal web applications
- Web applications
- Web applications by other providers
- Mobile applications
- Mobile applications by other providers

This is already a long list and we can expect it to grow in the future with new devices appearing, accompanied by different usage patterns.

Hexagonal architecture

So how can we make sure an application is ready to evolve? With the appearance and dominance of web applications, developers have realized that there is a split between what an application is built to process and the interface and technologies it uses. This split is not a bad thing, as it can be used to establish APIs at those points and encapsulate the business domain that the core concept domain-driven design is all about. One possible technique to accomplish this is known as **Hexagonal architecture**.

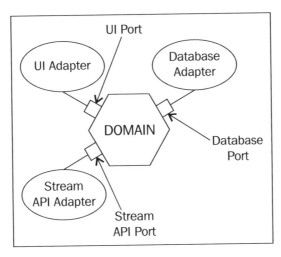

The application as a whole is seen as a hexagon, with the business domain located inside. While the business domain only cares about its own language and concepts, it uses ports to talk to whatever it needs. Ports are the interfaces to the outside world and establish a clear API for what is needed and how it should be provided. On the other hand, there are adapters, that is, elements providing the API. This gives a lot of flexibility, and it not only allows you to swap adapters, for example during a test, but to also try out different technologies more quickly to find the one that fits best, not by guessing but actually trying it with the application.

Applying the pattern

As an avid reader will have realized, our dungeon management application does not differ a lot from the booking application just described. Moving forward, we also want to integrate it with multiple UIs and other applications. Also, our business concepts are complex enough to make us reach for domain-driven design, so a Hexagonal architecture suits us well. But how do we get there?

This first thing to realize is that so far we have already been designing for it. Our core functionality is understood outside the context of a database or a web framework. The idea of hexagonal architecture and domain-driven design integrate very well after all. We now move forward to have a clear separation of what the business domain contains and what the outside provides. This is also referred to as **persistence ignorance**, as we want our domain to ignore the layers dealing with saving and loading data. As part of this pattern, we create separate objects or modules that encapsulate the actions of our domain, and use those to integrate into web frameworks as well as exposing as an API when we need to in the future.

Abstractions are not free; depending on the application, abstracting the data layers too much can introduce a performance overhead that might be too much to cope with. On the other hand, if your domain interacts with the data layer at such a frequency, there is possibly a problem in the domain itself and you might want to rethink your aggregates in the domain layer. The way we have to think about such patterns is more like a slider than a Boolean; we can increase and decrease the abstractions depending on the domain as well as the needs of our application's performance.

Plugging in a framework

So how can we go about making this work for our application? The first version we are going to build is set out to have a web UI, so we need to have to plug in a web framework so we don't have to reinvent the wheel. Node.js provides many options there, the most popular being `express.js`, which we've already used, so what we want to do is let express do what it does best, serving requests, while our core domain processes the logic for those requests.

Let's take a look at an example:

```
app.post("/prisoner_transfer", function(req, res) {
  var dungeon = Dungeon.findById(req.params.dungeonId)
  var prisoner = Prisoner.findById(req.params.prisonerId)

  prisonerTransfer(prisoner, dungeon, function(err) {
    var message
    if(err) {
      res.statusCode = 400
      message = { error: err.message }
    } else {
      res.statusCode = 201
      message = { success: true }
    }
    res.end(JSON.stringify(message))
  })
})
```

The code to manage the prisoner transfer is nicely encapsulated in its own module and only interacts with the domain objects. The other question is where the code should live. At this early stage, code like this might still validly reside in an `index.js` file, providing the interface, but as our project moves along we might move towards a more modular architecture containing the glue code that connects the domain to the express framework in its own module. At this stage, we might even create a middleware layer to inject dependencies automatically as we need them.

Summary

In this chapter, we got started with the project and are well on our way. We have everything in place to make the project progress and make it ready for changes that will no doubt follow. Again, the main idea has all been about isolation and making sure we think and tackle the domain, while not getting lost in the intricacies of language and frameworks and alike along the way.

As most programmers will agree, integrating systems and modeling data are two tasks that really require attention just to themselves, and with this setup, we are taking an important step towards this integration. Meanwhile, the architecture sets us up to keep modeling the data as we started out previously.

In the next chapter, we go into more detail on the domain objects themselves and what modeling them means in domain-driven design terms. We will be introducing the terminology to classify those models and drive them out using domain-driven design in conjunction with object orientation.

4
Modeling the Actors

We are now ready to dive head first into development, and we have a solid structure in place to help us deal with the arising changes that will come no matter what. It is time to think more about what the different components of our system are and how they interact.

Interaction in systems happens on multiple levels. The operating system interacts with the language runtime, the runtime interacts with our code, and then inside our code we create objects calling back out and calling other processes and so on. We have already seen how our domain objects can interact with the underlying framework and we can imagine how the code calls different libraries. When structuring interactions, it is important to know about the seams that exist and to create new ones where necessary. When calling other code, it is pretty clear where our code ends and where the library code starts. When we are creating code, it is easy to muddle responsibilities, but the better we can separate them, the better we can evolve our code in the future.

Almost all aspects of computer science deal with interactions between different components in some way or other, and so multiple techniques exist to make sure those interactions work well. In this chapter, we are focusing on the actors of the system and their interactions, and will go into the details of:

- Using object-oriented programming techniques to model domain actors
- Testing domain objects in isolation
- Identifying and naming roles in the domain

The shoulders of giants

One of the best known models of how interactions can be modeled and worked on is the **OSI/ISO** model that describes the interaction of layers in the networking stack. It comprises seven layers, each with a well-defined interface to be communicated with by the layer above, and to communicate with the layer below. Furthermore, each layer defines a protocol that allows it to communicate with a layer of the same level. With this in place, there is a very clear API to communicate with the layer and it is also clear how the layer can call back out to the system, therefore making it easy to replace parts of the system. The following diagram shows this how it is described in the OSI/ISO model. Each layer is defined by a protocol that allows instances on each side to communicate at their layer, as we move up the stack protocols are wrapped and unwrapped by the given instances:

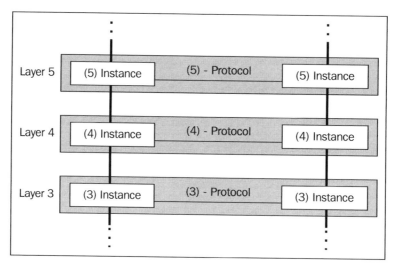

This model has not been adopted across the board of course, with TCP/IP focusing on five layers, and it has even been stated that too much layering can be considered harmful. But even those who are not in favor of the OSI/ISO model consider the basic idea valuable, and isolating communication is one of the basics of making the Internet work, so to speak. Each layer is replaceable, be it completely or just for a specific case, which is a powerful thing to have in any system.

Bringing this over to the world of modeling applications means that our objects should communicate at their layer in the business domain. In terms of domain-driven design, it is okay for an aggregate to interact with other aggregates to fulfill its purpose, but it is not okay for a service to reach into a entity without considering the aggregate. Reaching into different parts of an application without considering the appropriate APIs causes coupling two models together. In our dungeon, having a dungeon master of a foreign dungeon communicate directly with a prisoner is also a bad idea, marking the prisoner as a spy and getting him killed immediately, most likely. This not only causes problems due to tight coupling, but also opens the application up to security problems. There have been many instances of, for example, SQL injection attacks because a model accessing the database reached directly for the data passed in an HTTP request without a layer to mitigate the access.

Communication like this, where one object communicates with another part of the object graph, ignoring the gating interfaces, is a well understood problem and is solidified as the *Law of Demeter*, which states:

> *Each unit should have only limited knowledge about other units: only units "closely" related to the current unit.*

> *– Law of Demeter*

Often this is paraphrased in object-oriented language to say that a method should only have one dot. Having a method like the following on the orc master for example, violates this. The following code shows implementing an accessor for the available weapons in a dungeon, by reaching far into the objects controlled by the dungeon and its descendants:

```
function weapons() {
  result = []
  dungeon.orcs.forEach(function (orc) {
    result.push(orc.weapon.type)
  })
  return result
}
```

In this case, the orc master reaches each orc via its dungeon and asks it directly for the type of his weapon. This binds the orc master not only to the inner implementation of the dungeon, but also the orc and even the weapon itself; if any of those elements change, the method has to change as well. This not only makes the object itself harder to change, but the system overall is more rigid now and not as malleable under refactoring.

Code like the preceding is imperative in its operation on the data structures, where object-oriented code focuses on a more declarative style to reduce the amount of coupling. Declarative means the code tells objects what needs to be done and lets them handle the operations needed to achieve the goal:

> *Procedural code gets information then makes decisions. Object-oriented code tells objects to do things.*

> — *Alec Sharp*

Communication should not cross boundaries randomly, but in a well-defined and reasonable way to keep software malleable. This also means that when developing software, we need to be aware of the components and interfaces, identifying them as we have done already, and be aware as new ones arise from the code we are writing. The same is true for commands and events that represent messages being sent in our domain.

Even when thinking about the software under development very intensively beforehand and drawing diagrams like we have done, it is almost inevitable you'll miss certain abstractions that become clear when development has started. The code and the test we write should make the interfaces clear, and to take advantage of this fact a common way is to exercise the code under development as early as possible, and let it "tell" you about its dependents.

The Different approaches to development

Now that we are writing the code to solve problems in our domain, we can approach problems in different ways: one way is to start at the topmost level we have so far discovered and let this guide us down to our lower level objects and abstractions, or we can start with the components we identified, flush them out and build up the system. Both approaches are valid and are commonly referred to as "outside-in" or "inside-out" development. The advantage of inside-out is that we always have a running working system because we build the dependents first and build up the system. The disadvantage being that it is easier to lose sight of the bigger picture and get lost in the details.

What is common to the approaches is that they follow a style based on test-driven development. We are building the tests to let us guide the design and show us when we are done. We start using our code first to get a feel for how it would behave later, and implement what we think the behavior should be. This can be done by first focusing on the small, easier to grasp components to gain confidence in them, as it is done in the *inside-out* approach. Another way to approach it is to ask the big questions at the start, drilling down into more detail as we move along, as in the *outside-in* approach.

For this project, it feels more appropriate to start on the outside because we explored and got a feel for what the stakeholders want, but are not so clear about the exact components and their behavior; after all we are in a world we are not entirely familiar with. Especially in an unfamiliar world, we are very prone to start building pieces we never needed. Right now we don't know a lot about the messaging system between dungeons for example. We could start trying to build an abstraction here and allow us to control as much as possible, but, on the other hand, it might turn out that we only send one message a week and having this pop up on the dungeon master's screen to have him do it by hand is perfectly reasonable. In these kinds of evaluations, we have to keep in mind that our overarching goal should always be to deliver value and save money, and that can mean *not* building things. So how can we go about creating software without the underlying structure being in place?

Introducing mocks

When trying to model a system from the outside in, there is a need have objects stand in for what is eventually going to be the lower level implementation. This happens on every level and the concept of modeling the API first trickles down to the lower layers. We previously started building the prisoner transfer service, with dependency being on the prisoner and a dungeon; those again will have dependents that, when flushing out the objects, will need to be designed in similar ways.

The objects that enable this are called **mocks**; they are objects that provide a static implementation of a certain concept and can assert that they are called correctly. Mocks implement the protocol a certain object should follow. In a dynamic language, such as JavaScript, this is both easy and hard. Different JavaScript testing frameworks approach this differently; some use mock objects as described, while some provide spies that call through to the real object but monitor those calls for correctness. Both approaches work well and there are advantages to each.

 More information on spies can be found at `http://derickbailey.com/2014/04/23/mock-objects-in-nodejs-tests-with-jasmine-spies/`.

Creating a mock can be a simple as:

```
var myMock = {
  called: false,
  aFunction: function () { myMock.called = true }
}
```

Even though this is not a very advanced mock, it contains what we need. This object can now stand in for anything that requires the specific API of providing a function called aFunction. It is also possible to check whether a function has been called by checking the called variable after the test has been run. These checks can be done with the assert library provided directly by the runtime without the need for additional testing frameworks. In the following code, we use our very simple mock we created above to assert that a function is indeed called at a given time:

```
var assert = require("assert")

function test_my_mock() {
  mock = Object.create(myMock) // called on the mock is false
  mock.aFunction()
  assert(mock.called) // called on the mock is true
}

test_my_mock()
```

In this case, we use the Object.create method to create a new instance of our myMock object, exercise it, and verify it worked correctly.

How to create mock objects is quite specific to the circumstances when they are needed and multiple libraries implement their creation. One library that is quite commonly used is **Sinon.JS,** and it provides many different ways to verify functionality, implement stubs, mocks, and spies. Combined with Mocha as our testing framework, we can create a mock test by creating the object we want to mock and letting Sinon.JS mock due the heavy lifting of verification for us. We can now describe the behavior of the API in very readable terms, using the combined features of Mocha to provide the behavioral descriptions and Sinon.JS to provide advanced mocking and verification. Here's an example of this:

```
var sinon = require("sinon")

var anApi = {
  foo: function () {
      return "123"
      }
}

describe("Implementing an API", function () {
  it("is a mock", function () {
    var mock = sinon.mock(anApi)
    mock.expects("foo").once()
```

```
    anApi.foo()
    mock.verify()
  })
})
```

The concept of a mock on the surface is quite simple, but its usage can be difficult as it can be hard to discover where the right place for a mock actually is.

 For more information on mocks, visit `http://www.mockobjects.com/2009/09/brief-history-of-mock-objects.html`.

Why and why not to mock

Our initial description had focused too much on implementation, the critical idea was that the technique emphasizes the roles that objects play for each other.

A Brief History of Mock Objects – Steve Freeman

Mock objects stand in for other objects in a system during testing, and sometimes even during development. There are multiple reasons to do this, for example, the underlying structure is not implemented yet, or the call would be really expensive both in a cost of time during development or even in money calling to an API that charges by the amount of calls. For developers it can be very convenient to be able to run the tests offline as well, and there are more reasons why somebody would want to not call the real system but something in its place.

This kind of practice is normally referred to as **stubbing out** an external dependency. When combined with making assertions about this dependency, this stub becomes a mock, which is often helpful during development to ensure that some code is called correctly, at the right time and, of course, when testing.

It is very easy to fall into the trap of creating very specific mock objects, mocking inner dependencies of other objects, and so forth. The important thing to keep in mind is that a mock should always represent a role in the system. Various other objects in the real world can play this role, but they can be represented in one mock. In classical object-oriented terms, this would mean that we are mocking interfaces not classes. In JavaScript, there are no interfaces so we need to select the right objects to mock. The object, or part of the object that is our mock, needs to only represent what is essential to the test, and nothing more. This comes naturally when we drive our design through tests, but we need to keep an eye on this as the software evolves and changes, as changes might result in our tests overspecifying an object through a mock.

Who is involved in the prisoner transfer?

In the previous sections, we did a lot of exploring in the domain to get a view of what has to be done to make actions in the system happen. With this knowledge, we can now get a clear-cut concept of how a prisoner transfer should happen. The tests we created earlier specify some behavior and collaborators we are aware of in the domain. We represent them as basic JavaScript objects that contain the properties necessary to satisfy the tests; we, for example, know that a dungeon needs a message inbox to be notified, but we don't know any properties for the prisoner yet. The following code provides some simple functions to let us describe the type of object we are using, as the code grows and our knowledge of what makes a prisoner or a dungeon gets solidified we can fill those out to continue to be stand-ins for the respective objects during our tests:

```
/* get a prisoner to transfer */
function getPrisonerForTransfer() { return {} }

/* get a dungeon to transfer to */
function getDungenonToTransfer() { return { inbox: [] } }
```

So far, the prisoner as well as the dungeon are specific JavaScript objects created just to represent what we need at this moment. Looking further into the details, other actors are involved as well, namely the orc guarding the prisoner along the way, as well as the transfer carriage. Of course, those again have dependencies: the carriage consists of the driver, the wooden carriage working as a mobile cell for the prisoner, as well as the horses that pull it. All those pieces are potentially scarce resources that we need to acquire. Here is where domain modeling comes in again; in the context of our application we can stay away from looking at them as separate things because if either is missing the whole object won't be able to function. We can focus on which roles the different objects play and acquire them as aggregates where it fits our model.

Different objects and their roles

The carriage is one of those described roles; we do not care at this moment what the carriage consists of but treat it as one thing that fulfills some purpose in our system. The carriage as a whole is an aggregate we only want to inspect from the outside for now and don't care much about its internals. Right there, the carriages public API shows a seam that that we need to account for when we model. We might care about horses being a separate thing later, for example, to model a messenger where we want to allocate horses for both carriages as well as messengers.

An aggregate is not a way to limit the share ability of resources but a concept to make dealing with the comprised object less complex. It does not change the fact that a carriage without horses is useless, and that something else also might need to acquire horses as a resource. The carriage is a role in our system. It provides a public API and takes care of its own internal data and dependencies. It is an aggregate in itself on a smaller scale.

The idea to discover such seams is a fundamental idea when it comes to building systems using mocks and stubs. By mocking out roles in the system, we can interact with the role before it really exists and explore its functionality without being hampered by the internal implementation.

Naming objects according to the domain

There are only two hard things in Computer Science: cache invalidation and naming things.

– Phil Karlton

When exploring roles in a domain, the most complicated thing is most often the fact that we need to name the role that we try to establish in the system. When we are able to name a thing, we can naturally associate it with the role it plays in a system. When building a software system and being able to point out the roles by giving them concrete names, we make it easy for every developer working on the system to know where to put functionality related to the part they need to work on.

Previously, we introduced the concept of a carriage, comprising the cart itself, horses to tow it, and a driver. This is one example of naming a concept according to the domain. In the world of the orc dungeons, the concept of a carriage is very clear, and what is needed to run it is very clear. By using the language of the stakeholders in the system, we are increasing the teams' language and enabling all the stakeholders to participate. We saw this before when identifying the parts of the domain; we now make sure we continue to increase the language while creating abstractions. This allows us to hide certain details behind a common role.

The traps of common names like *Manager

The carriage we introduced a concept, well known in the domain, is a good abstraction to have; as software developers, however, we are prone to keep reusing elements we have seen before in other applications. When naming roles, it is very easy to fall into a pattern of naming. Very often, we see `Manager` objects that really only exist for the lack of a better name about the role they fulfill:

```
var transportManager = new TransportManager(driver, horse, cart)
transportManager.initializeTransport(prisoner)
```

Even though this object fulfills the same responsibility as the object we named `carriage` before, finding out what it does is no longer obvious by the name. Even though it is clear to the developers on the team what this object is meant to do, the other stakeholders will be confused. This drives a separation in the team and will not foster involvement in the development process by non-developers.

Naming an object as a manager often means naming it after what it does at this moment instead of the role it fulfills in the system in general. Naming an object this way makes it hard to abstract away the details within it. To know what a `Manager` object does always means knowing what it is managing and how its internal details work to make sense of it. The abstraction leaks to other parts of the system, and everybody using the manager will look into the parts it is managing and the details.

The pain of manager objects often becomes very clear in the context of writing tests. When we want to test a manager and we don't see a clear abstraction, we need to care about the internal dependencies and therefore need to hold on to them in our tests. This makes tests look complicated and the setup starts to trump the actual assertion part. With objects named after generic roles, we get objects serving the purpose of very generic roles and therefore move away from domain-specific objects. This can cause pain as those generic objects are only made specific by their internal implementation, and therefore are bad representatives of the role they are supposed to play.

[When you have trouble coming up with a name for an object, try naming it something obviously silly first and let the exploration of the domain guide you to a more specific and meaningful name.]

Readability of method names

In **Object-oriented Programming (OOP)**, an object holds data and is responsible for the actions most closely related to the data it holds. Functions operating on the data, such as computing new data from the internal state of the object, are called queries. Examples for such a function are ones that compute compound data, like the full name of an orc from its set first name and last name:

```
function Orc(firstName, lastName) {
  this.firstName = firstName
  this.lastName = lastName
}

Orc.prototype.fullName = function () {
  return this.firstName + " " + this.lastName
}
```

On the other hand, if an object is not immutable, there need to be functions to modify its internal state. Functions that change the internal state of an object are called commands; they allow external objects to send commands to the object to change its behavior. The following is an example of this:

```
function Orc(age) {
  this.age = age
  this.attacking = false
}

Orc.prototype.goToBattle = function () {
  if (age < 18) throw new Error("To young for battle")
  this.attacking = true
}
```

As commands change their internal state, it needs to be very clear what is happening and the object should have as much control as possible over what to actually do in the case of the command, so the command tells the object what to do and does not ask it for its state to modify it. Making this happen means we want to instruct the object to accomplish a task, without inspecting its properties. The opposite is checking object properties and based on those, making a decision in place of the object responsible for the properties. The *Tell, Don't Ask* principle is an important principle of OOP. The preceding example follows this concept, by not creating a setter to *attack* the property, we make sure the Orc object is in control of its internal state. Making domain-specific commands read like what they do, instead of creating an extensive amount of setter/getter methods, helps readability as well as making sure that the state is well managed. In object orientation, we want the object to be responsible for its state and the methods that operate on that state.

Not only are the objects part of a consistent naming scheme that allows us to model the domain. When we are modeling functionality and we want it to read clearly, we need to make the method names readable as well. In the previous example, the `TransportManager` only method is `initializeTransport` and it more or less repeats the name of the object. This pattern is very common when objects are `Managers` or `Executors`, or alike, but it does not help readability. This is the same trap as creating setters that are called outside the context of setting a value to initialize the object. The method needs to tell what the command does.

An object named after a role in the system allows much better readability of methods. The domain name `Carriage` makes the method name `transport` much more understandable because it comes naturally with the concept of a carriage in the domain.

With all this, it now comes the point where we need to think about how we model the objects to ease testing as well as development.

Objects first

When building the dungeon manager, we set out to create a maintainable and evolvable piece of software. The core principles of OOP are there to help us out when dealing with objects, but JavaScript is special when it comes to object orientation.

As many JavaScript programmers will most certainly have heard, JavaScript uses prototypical inheritance and, more importantly, has not really got a concept of classes, only instances.

 Even though the next version of JavaScript, **ECMAScript 6**, introduces the class `keyword`, the core language design does not change. Classes are really just syntactic sugar over the prototypical inheritance present in JavaScript right now. If you want to know more about ES6, follow the blog http://www.2ality.com/ by Alex Rauschmayer, who describes and follows the evolving JavaScript language closely.

Of course, this does not make JavaScript the worst language to perform the task we are trying to achieve because this lack does not limit the power of the language in any way, but really makes it a superset of classical object-oriented languages.

Let's first do a quick recap of how object orientation works in JavaScript and how we can use the power of the language to help us out in modeling the system that we have been drafting out so far.

The basics of objects in JavaScript

In Object-oriented languages such as Ruby or even Java, objects are based on classes. Even though it might be possible to create a plain object, it is not the norm. Taking Ruby as an example to create an object with a method like our carriage, you would write something like:

```
class Carriage
  def transport prisoner
    # some work happens
  end
end

carriage = Carriage.new
carriage.transport(a_prisoner)
```

In JavaScript, for very simple objects and also, very importantly, for the tests, we don't need to have a class first to have an object like this:

```
var carriage = {
  transport: function(prisoner) {
    // do some work
  }
}

carriage.transport(aPrisoner)
```

The preceding code will do the same thing without the necessity of creating a class along with the object first. This can be very powerful especially when modeling a new API, because it allows very lightweight usage and generation during this phase of development.

Besides the availability of plain objects that are constructed via { }, JavaScript allows functions to be used as objects. Using functions as object constructors means very much the same flexibility as classes in classical object orientation would. Functions in JavaScript are objects that encapsulate their internal state and the state of any variables they reference at the time of their creation from the outside world. Due to those properties, functions in JavaScript are the basic building blocks to be used to create objects, and special support via the keyword new is part of the language:

```
function Carriage() {}
Carriage.prototype.transport = function (prisoner) {
  // do some work
}

var carriage = new Carriage()
carriage.transport(aPrisoner)
```

This looks a lot like the Ruby code and behaves very similarly to it. Constructors are a special beast in JavaScript and much has been written about their usage or non-usage. In a lot of cases, the idea of a class of objects being related by common functionality is a good idiom to use, and modern JavaScript engines were built with this is mind. So don't fear constructors, but be aware of their special use of the keyword new and the confusion they might cause around new developers.

 A lot has been written about the problems with new in JavaScript. For more information and the best information about the internals of JavaScript as a language, read *JavaScript: The Good Parts, Douglas Crockford, O'Reilly.*

Inheritance and why you won't need it

Of course, just the construction of classes and their usage is only a part of being an OO (object-oriented) language. Especially in Java, it is very common to build quite complex inheritance hierarchies that allow common functionality to be shared across objects.

The basic concept of inheritance is that all the methods of the parent are also available on the child.

Modeling patterns beyond inheritance

Favor 'object composition' over 'class inheritance'.

– Gang of Four 1995:20

Even though inheritance is possible in JavaScript, it is not necessarily the best route to go down for designing when an application like it is stated in the *Gang of Four*. Inheritance creates a very strong bond between the parent class and its children; this in itself means a leak of knowledge in parts of the system that it should not. Inheritance is the strongest possible form of coupling between two objects, and coupling itself should always be a very deliberate choice. Deep inheritance trees quickly make a piece of software very resistant to change as the changes tend to ripple through the whole system. There is a bigger problem so as well—as JavaScript does not do compile time checking of the interface and relationships, it is easier for those parts to get out of sync, and cause bugs in the system, than in more static languages.

For those reasons, and also due to the fact that classical inheritance is rarely needed in a dynamic language like JavaScript, inheritance is almost never used. There are other patterns that have been hinted at already to counter the need for inheritance.

The object composition

What can we do when we don't want to share functionality via inheritance? The easiest way to go is to pass the object that already implements the functionality we need and use it directly, for example:

```
function Notifications(store) {
  if (typeof(store) === 'undefined') {
    this.store = []
  } else {
    this.store = store
  }
}

Notifications.prototype.add = function (notification) {
  store.push(notifictation)
}
```

A notification is a very simple object that manages the notifications for a part of the system; it does not concern itself greatly with how notifications are saved for later processing but simply delegates this to a store object that by default is implemented as an array.

Delegating to native types is normally done a lot, but this for all other objects that are created by the programmer. Composition like this has the big advantage that it eases testing especially when the dependencies are passed in, like in the example just given, we can simply replace the store object in our tests with something that ensures the right calls have been made.

Polymorphism without inheritance

When I see a bird that walks like a duck and swims like a duck and quacks like a duck, I call that bird a duck.

– Michael Heim

Another reason for inheritance in languages such as Java is the need for polymorphism. The idea is that a method should be implemented differently in different objects. In classical inheritance combined with type checking, this means that the objects on which the method is called need to have a common ancestor or interface because the type checker will complain otherwise:

```
interface Orc {
    abstract public String kill(String attacker);
}

class SwordMaster implements Orc {
    public String kill(String name) {
        return "Slash " + name;
    }
}

class AxeMaster implements Orc {
    public String kill(String name) {
        return "Split " + name;
    }
}
```

Now we can pass both a `SwordMaster` class or an `AxeMaster` class to somebody in need in order for an orc to guard them:

```
class Master {
  Orc[] guards;
  public Master(Orc[] guards) {
    this.guards = guards;
  }

  public void figthOfAttack(String[] attackers) {
    for(int i = 0; i < attackers.length; i++) {
      System.out.println(guards[i].kill(attackers[i]));
    }
  }
}
```

This kind of overhead is not needed in a language that supports duck typing. In JavaScript, we can just write this without the need for an interface, both orcs can just be plain JavaScript objects, as shown in the following example:

```
var axeMaster = {
  kill: function(name) { return "Hack " + name; }
}

var swordMaster = {
  kill: function(name) { return "Slash " + name; }
}
```

The `Master` object being guarded can now just call the method needed on each guard without the need for a matching type:

```
var Master = function (guards) { this.guards = guards }
Master.prototype.fightOfAttackers = function (attackers) {
  var self = this
  attackers.forEach(function (attacker, idx) {
    console.log(self.guards[idx].kill(attacker))
  })
}
```

Duck typing means that an object is defined by what it can do rather than what it is. We already saw this behavior when building our own very simple mocks. As long as the method is defined on the object, it doesn't matter what its type is when we call it, so there is really no need to have a common ancestor.

Due to the very dynamic nature of JavaScript and the availability of duck typing, the need for inheritance is very much obviated.

Applying object design to the domain

With an understanding of conceptual object design, we need to apply all the concepts to our domain. We continue modeling the prisoner transfer we started. So far, we have an entry point to the application module that will ultimately handle this. From the tests, we know that the prisoner transfer relies on a prisoner and a dungeon object.

Building a system on simple objects

So let's walk through what the prisoner transfer needs to do and what its collaborators are. Previously, we identified that the prisoner transfer will need a prisoner, obviously, and a target dungeon to transfer to, and the prisoner transfer should manage everything else. It is important to think about what the minimal input is from a user perspective to limit the API surface.

Of course the prisoner transfer, which is a service in DDD speak, needs more collaborators to really fulfill its purpose. First is a reference to the local dungeon to acquire resources such as orcs to act as keepers, carriages to move the prisoner, and possibly more. A goal of a managed transfer is also to notify the other dungeon, so we also need the means to notify them.

As we found out in the previous chapters, the concept of notifications is not well understood yet, so for now we can assume that there will be a service that allows us to send a message to a target, for a specific reason. We can program against the abstraction of a messaging service, allowing us to further specify what we are going to need out of the system. Bringing all this together and flushing it out brings us to the following:

```
prisonerTransfer = function (prisoner,
                             otherDungeon,
                             ourDungeon,
                             notifier,
                             callback) {
  var keeper = ourDungeon.getOrc()
  var carriage = ourDungeon.getCarriage()
  var transfer = prepareTransfer(carriage, keeper, prisoner)
  if (transfer) {
    notifier.message(dungeon, transfer)
    callback()
  } else {
    callback(new Error("Transfer initiation failed."))
  }
}
function prepareTransfer(carriage, keeper, prisoner) {
  return {}
}
```

All calls are just simple calls to objects that can have a stand-in of a simple plain JavaScript object during the tests:

```
it("notifies other dungeons of the transfer", function (done) {
  prisonerTransfer("prisoner",
                   getOtherDungeon(),
                   getLocalDungeon(),
                   getNotifier(),
                   function (err) {
    assert.ifError(err)
    assert.equal(dungeon.inbox.length, 1)
    done()
  })
})
```

Returning plain objects with the functionality needed, which we will ultimately make their own modules based on the design being mocked up now, is all there is to creating the roles of the collaborators:

```
function getOtherDungeon() {
  return { inbox: [] }
}

function getLocalDungeon() {
  return {
    getOrc: function () { return {} },
      getCarriage: function () { return {} }
      }
    }

function getNotifier() {
  return {
    message: function (target, reason) { target.inbox.push({}) }
    }
  }
```

This top-level design really brings us along the way to create the underlying functionality. We can already see very clearly what we need from a notification system, and flushing out the transfer itself to perform its duties will tell us a lot more about the other collaborators as well.

Summary

After reading this chapter, you have a solid foundation on how we can model the prisoner transfer inside the system. We used a very simple design with the least amount of tooling overhead possible. Our system leverages the dynamic nature of JavaScript to create simple stubs for objects we haven't created, yet, and we were able to validate the first understanding we discussed in our previous research.

In the next chapter, we are going to further explore the other roles in the system. We focus on classifying them in domain-driven design terms so we can reuse the patterns explored by others in the space. We are also going to focus more on the language to foster further communication and how it can work with those patterns to allow very clear communication in the domain.

5

Classification and Implementation

According to an IBM study (`http://www-935.ibm.com/services/us/gbs/bus/pdf/gbe03100-usen-03-making-change-work.pdf`), only 41% of projects meet their schedule, budget, and quality goals. The success or failure of a project largely does not depend on the technology, but the people involved.

Imagine a software project where every developer is always aware of all the intricacies of the decision making process that goes into every part of a project. In this ideal world, a developer could always make an informed decision and provided no developer wants to actively harm the project, the decisions will be reasonable. If an incorrect decision is made, it will not cause a huge problem in the grand scheme of things because the developer who touches this part of the project next will know what to do to fix it and will also be aware of all the dependencies involved. Such a project is highly unlikely to fail from a project perspective. The sad truth, though, is that there are almost no such projects in the world, and this is most likely due to the overhead such a system would create by needing the whole team to review every change made.

This might work for a very small project, most likely a start-up with few engineers, but it simply does not scale up as the project grows. When functionality and complexity grow, we need to decompose the project, and as we have seen already, small projects are easier to handle than big ones. Decomposition is not easy, so we need to find the seams in the project, and we also need to be aware of and decide on a governance model for the project as a whole, as well as the sub-projects, or sub-domains in it.

In the open source world, the Linux kernel project is a good example of a project starting out with only a few developers and growing since then. Since increasing beyond a size that one person can keep in their head at any point in time, the kernel has split into sub-projects, or sub-domains, be it the network handling, or filesystem, or others. Each sub-project has established its own domain, and the project grows with the trust that each sub-project will do the right thing. This means that the projects will drift apart, so an open mailing list enables discussions on topics around the grand architecture and the goal of the project in general. To facilitate this, the language used in this mailing list is very focused on the needs of the community. Explaining everything in detail every time would otherwise end up in huge discussions that completely miss the point.

In this chapter, we will go into detail on how we can leverage domain-driven design in the context of a growing project, in particular:

- Using and extending the language of the project
- Managing the context of the domain and its sub-domains
- The building blocks of a domain-driven project, aggregates, entities, value-objects, and services

Building a common language

We can't make every developer constantly aware of the project as a whole, but we can make the decisions very clear and the structure very intuitive to use through the establishment of a common language that is shared inside the project. A developer who looks at a piece of unfamiliar code should be able to figure out what it does and where it belongs in the system's context as a whole, if they are familiar with the language used throughout the project. Even as a project grows in a domain and the language of the sub-domain becomes more pronounced and starts to focus more on the specific parts of the sub-domain it is used in, it is important to keep an overall structure in place. As a developer of one sub-domain, I should not feel lost looking at a separate sub-domain as the language of the overarching domain maintains a global context for me to follow.

We have been building a common language so far by taking words from the business domain and using them in the application. A business expert is able to broadly understand what each component is about, and how the components will interact. It is also important to build this language as we grow, with developers contributing new words to the business domain to disambiguate elements.

These kinds of contributions are not only valuable to developers, as they are now able to clearly communicate what a certain element is, they are also beneficial for business experts as they can now communicate more clearly as well. If a term fits well, it will be adapted by the domain; if it does not, then it is better to drop it in most cases. To do this, we must first be make ourselves aware of what kind of patterns are available to us and use the terms already provided to us to let them influence the language we use throughout.

The importance of object classification

Developers like to classify things, as we saw earlier when describing why naming things like `SomethingManager` is harmful. We like to classify things because it gives us a way to make assumptions about the object we are dealing with. Describing the purpose of a certain element is not only problematic and error-prone in the business domain, but also in the programming domain. We want to be able to quickly associate certain parts of the code with certain problems. While a ubiquitous language solves this part in the business domain, we can draw from patterns to better describe our programming problems. Let's take a look at an example:

Developer 1: Hi, let's talk about the code to transform between our domain objects and the persistence.

Developer 2: Yes, I think there is a lot of room to optimize here. Have we ever looked at something provided by an outside company here?

Developer 1: Yes, we have, but we have very special needs and the common available alternatives seem to be not performing well enough for us.

Developer 2: Oh, okay. I was under the impression our home grown version has trouble with threading and is overall not that performant.

Developer 1: I don't think we need to talk about threading here, this should be handled at a lower level.

Developer 2: Wait, are we not talking about the database connection here? How much lower do you want to get?

Developer 1: No, no! I'm talking about the transformation of domain objects to database objects as we translate the fields to the right types and the column names and so on.

Developer 2: Oh, in this case you are talking to the wrong person. I'm not familiar with this part, sorry.

This conversation is likely to happen when bad naming creeps into a project. Developer 1 is talking about what would commonly be known as a **Data Mapper Pattern**, while Developer 2 is talking about the database API. Having commonly accepted names not only eases the conversation, but also lets certain developers much more easily express which part of the code they are more or less familiar with.

Patterns are most commonly used for naming programming techniques, for example, the Data Mapper Pattern describes a way to deal with the interaction between objects and their persistence to a database.

 A Data Mapper performs a bidirectional transfer of data between a persistent data store and the in-memory data representation of domain objects or data structures like it. It was named in *Patterns of Enterprise Application Architecture, Martin Fowler, Pearson.*

In domain-driven design, we also have *certain* way of dealing with certain kinds of objects and their relationships. On the one hand, there are patterns for organizing the development itself, and on the other hand there are names given to objects that fulfill a specific purpose. This kind of classification is what this chapter is all about. We build an understanding of certain domain elements by making them into concrete implementations of certain domain-driven design concepts.

Seeing the bigger picture

When dealing with a large project, the most common problem is to figure out what the guiding idea behind the design is. When a piece of software grows large, it is likely that the project comprises of more than one project but is actually split into sub-projects, each responsible for its own API and design. In terms of domain-driven design, there are domains and sub-domains. Each sub-domain carries its own context; in domain-driven design this is the bounded-context. The separate contexts together with the relationship of the main domain and its sub-domains hold the knowledge together in a conclusive whole.

On the server side, there is a move towards service-oriented architecture, which introduces quite a hard split between certain elements of the project by separating them out into different components that are run separately.

In Java, there has always been the concept of packages that define their own visibility. JavaScript is somewhat lacking in this area as all the code is traditionally run in the browser under one thread. This does not mean of course that all is lost, as we can separate namespaces by convention and tools like **npm** and **browserify** now enable us to use backend like separation on the frontend as well.

Supporting the process of looking up certain parts of the code, as well as figuring out what can be shared in between different parts of the domain, is a problem that has been tackled in multiple ways by different languages. As JavaScript is very dynamic, it means that there has never been a strict way to enforce privacy of certain parts in the language itself, for example keywords such as `private`. It is, however, possible to hide certain details, if we choose to do so. The following code uses a JavaScript pattern to define private properties and functions in the object:

```
function ExaggeratingOrc(name) {
  var that = this
  // public property
  that.name = name

  // private property
  var realKills = 0
  // private method
  function killCount() {
    return realKills + 10
  }

  // public method using private method
  that.greet = function() {
    console.log("I am " + that.name + " and I killed " +
killCount())
  }

  // public method using private property
  that.kill = function() { // public
    realKills = realKills + 1
  }
}
```

```
var orc = new ExaggeratingOrc("Axeman Axenson")
orc.killCount() // => TypeError: Object #< ExaggeratingOrc> has no
method 'killCount'
orc.greet() // => I am Axeman Axenson and I killed 10
```

This style of coding is possible, but it is not very idiomatic. In JavaScript, programmers tend to trust their fellow programmers to do the right thing and assume that if somebody wants to gain access to a certain property, he or she will have a good reason for it.

 A great feature of object orientation often mentioned is that it hides the details of implementation from others. Depending of the environment you work in, the reason for hiding details is often different. While most Java developers go to great lengths to prevent others from touching "their" implementation. Most developers of JavaScript tend to interpret it as the fact that others developers shouldn't need to know how things work, but if they want to reuse internal parts they are free to do so and have to deal with the consequences. It is hard to say what works better in practice.

The same is true on a higher level of abstraction; it would be possible to hide a lot of details but in general, packages tend to be quite open to expansion exposing an inner structure if a programmer wants to get to it. JavaScript itself, and its culture, don't lend themselves nicely to hiding details effectively. We can go to great lengths to achieve this effect, but it would go against the principles people expect from the software.

Even though hiding many details completely is hard, we still need to maintain consistency in our application. This is what we use aggregates for, which encapsulate a set of functionality to expose through a coherent interface. For our domain-driven design, we need to be aware of this fact; by using the right language and patterns, we need to guide other programmers through our code. We want to provide the right context in the right situation by naming consistently and guiding the use of domain related names through tests explaining the level a certain piece of functionality is located at. When we classify certain parts of the software as an aggregate, we show the next developer that the safe way to access the functionality is through this aggregate. With this in mind, even though it is still possible to reach inside and inspect the inner details, you should only do this if you have a very good reason to do so.

Value objects

When dealing with objects in various languages, including JavaScript, objects are almost universally passed and compared by reference, which means that an object that is passed to a method does not get copied, but rather its pointer gets passed, and when two objects are compared, their pointers are compared. This is not how we think about objects and especially value objects, as we think of those as identical if their properties are identical. More importantly, we don't want to consider the inner implementation details when we consider things like equality. This has some implications for the function using the object; one important implication is that modifying the object will actually change it for everybody in the system, for example:

```
function iChangeThings(obj) {
  obj.thing = "changed"
}


obj = {}
obj.thing // => undefined
iChangeThings(obj)
obj.thing // => "changed"
```

Related to this is the fact that comparing does not always yield the expected result as in this case:

```
function Coin(value) {
  this.value = value
}

var fiftyCoin = new Coin(50)
var otherFiftyCoin = new Coin(50)

fiftyCoin == otherFiftyCoin // => false
```

Even though this might be obvious to us as programmers, it really is not capturing the intention of the objects in the domain. In the real world, having two 50-cent coins and considering them different is not convenient, for example, in the domain of payment. It does not make sense for a shop to accept a certain 50-cent coin while rejecting another. We would like to compare our coins by the value they represent, rather than the physical form. On the other hand, coin collectors will think quite differently about the problem, and for them a certain 50-cent coin might be worth a fortune, while a generic one is not. The comparison of objects and their identity always has to be considered in the context of the domain.

If we decide to compare and identify an object in a software system by its property value rather than its intrinsic identity, we have an instance of a value object.

The advantages of value objects

Objects that are passed around and can be modified can cause unexpected behavior, and depending on the domain, comparing objects by identity can be misleading. In those kind of situations, declaring a certain object as a value object can save you a lot of trouble down the road. Making sure an object is not modified in turn makes it easier to reason about any code interacting with it. This is because we don't have to look at the dependencies down the line, as we can just use the object as it is.

JavaScript has support for these kinds of objects built in; using the `Object.freeze` method will make sure that no changes can happen to the object after it has been frozen. Adding this to the construction of the object will let us be confident that the object will always behave as we expect it to. The following code constructs an immutable value object using `freeze`:

```
"use strict"

function Coin(value) {
  this.value = value
  Object.freeze(this)
}

function changeValue(coin) {
  coin.value = 100
}

var coin = new Coin(50)
changeValue(coin) // => TypeError: Cannot assign to read only
property 'value' of #<Coin>
```

A noteworthy addition to JavaScript was the `use strict` directive. If we do not use this directive, the assignment to the value property would silently fail. Even though we can still be sure that no changes will happen, this will cause some blank stares at the code. So even if it is mostly left out in this book in order to keep the code samples short, the use of `use strict` is highly recommended. You can use **JSLint** to enforce this, for example (`http://www.jslint.com/`).

When dealing with value objects, it is also a good idea to provide a function to compare them against each other, whatever that means in the current domain. In the coin example, we would want to compare them by the value of the coin, so we provide an `equals` function to do this:

```
Coin.prototype.equals = function(other) {
  if(!(other instanceof Coin)) {
    return false
  }

  return this.value === other.value
}
}

var notACoin = { value: 50 }
var aCoin = new Coin(50)
var coin = new Coin(50)

coin.equals(aCoin) // => true
coin.equals(notACoin) // => false
```

The `equals` function makes sure we are dealing with coins, and if so checks if they have the same value. This makes sense in the domain of payment, but might not necessarily hold true everywhere else. It is important to note that the fact something is a value object in a certain domain does not mean this is universally true. This becomes specifically important when dealing with the relationship of projects inside an organization. It can very well be necessary to have separate definitions of similar things because they are regarded in different ways across applications.

> The preceding code uses the __proto__ property of an object, which is an internally managed property pointing to the prototype of an object and was a recent addition to JavaScript. Even though this is very convenient, we can always get to the prototype via `Object.prototype(object)` if necessary and if __proto__ is not available.

Of course, just having a method to compare does not mean everybody will use it in all situations, and JavaScript does not provide a way to enforce it. This is one place where the domain language comes to save us. Spreading the knowledge about the domain will make it clear to fellow developers what should be considered a value object, and the ways to compare it. This might be a good idea in a situation where you are documenting the class in use and need to provide the next person with some details.

The referential transparency

The `Coin` objects we have been working with have another interesting property, which could be useful in our system, and this is that they are referentially transparent. This is a very fancy way of saying whenever we have a coin, it does not matter what we do with it, as it will be regarded as the same in every part of the application. We are therefore free to pass it to other functions and keep a hold of it without having to worry about it changing. We also don't need to follow the coin as a dependency, checking what might have happened to it before or how it might be changed by other functions in case we pass it along. The following code illustrates the simple usage of a coin object constructed as a value object. Even though the code depends on it we don't need to take special care of interacting with the object as it is defined as an immutable value object:

```
Orc.prototype.receivePayment = function (coin) {
  if (this.checkIfValid(coin)) {
    return this.wallet.add(coin)
  } else {
    return false
  }
}
```

While the preceding example is a save operation with only one dependency – the wallet, to watch with the `Coin` being a value object, it would be much more complicated if the `Coin` object is an entity. The `checkIfValid` function might change attributes and we would therefore have to investigate what happens inside.

Not only does the value object make the code flow easier to follow, referential transparency is a very important factor when it comes to dealing with caching objects across the lifetime of our application. Even though JavaScript is single-threaded, so we don't have to worry about objects being modified by other threads, we have seen that objects can still be modified by other functions, and they also might change for other reasons. With a value object, we never have to worry about this, so we are free to save it for later and refer to it whenever we need to. In between functions, an event might occur that leads to the modification of objects we are currently working with, and this can make it very hard to track down bugs. In the following code, we see a simple usage of the `EventEmitter` variable and how we can use it to listen to a `"change"` event:

```
var events = require("events")
var myEmitter = new events.EventEmitter()

var thing = { count: 0 }

myEmitter.on("change", function () {
  thing.count++
})
```

```
function doStuff(thing) {
  thing.count = 10
  process.nextTick(function() {
    doMoreStuff(thing)
  })
}

function doMoreStuff(thing) {
  console.log(thing.count)
}

doStuff(thing)
myEmitter.emit("change")
// => prints 11
```

Looking at just the functions doStuff and doMoreStuff, we would expect to see a 10 printed to the console, but it actually prints 11 as the event change is interleaved. This is pretty obvious in the previous example, but dependencies like this can hide deep inside the code, crossing many more functions. Value objects make the same mistake impossible, as the change to the object would have been prohibited. This is not the end to all errors in asynchronous programming, of course, and more patterns are needed to make sure this works as expected; for most use cases I would recommend a look at **async** (https://github.com/caolan/async), a library to help with all kinds of asynchronous programming tasks.

Objects defined as entities

As we have seen, having objects primarily defined by their properties can be really useful and helps us deal with a lot of scenarios when designing a system. So, we often see that certain objects have a different lifecycle attached to them. In such a case, the object is defined by its ID, and in domain-driven design terms, it is considered an entity. This is a contrast to value objects that are defined by their properties, and are considered to be equal when their properties match. An entity is only ever equal if it has the same ID, even if all the properties match; as long as the ID is different, the entity is not the same.

Entity objects manage the lifecycle inside the application; this can either be the lifecycle spread across the application as a whole, but it might well be a transaction happening in the system. In the dungeon, we are dealing with a lot OF cases where we don't really care about the lifecycle of an object itself, but rather WE care about its attributes. Staying with the prisoner transport example, we know that it comprises many different objects, but most of them could be implemented as value objects. We do not really care about the lifecycle of the orc guard accompanying the transport, and we are fine as long as we know there is one and that he is armed to protect us.

This might seem a little seem counterintuitive as we know we need to take care about the assignment of orcs as we don't have an infinite number of them, but really there are two separate concepts hiding inside, one being the `Orc` as a value object and the other being its assignment to guard the transport. The following code defines an `OrcRepository` function, which can be used to get orcs under controlled circumstances and use them. This pattern can be used to control access to a shared resource in conjunction with most likely database access encapsulated within:

```
function OrcRepository(orcs, swords) {
  this.orcs = orcs
  this.swords = swords
}

OrcRepository.prototype.getArmed = function () {
  if (this.orcs > 0 && this.swords > 0) {
    this.orcs -= 1
    this.swords -= 1
    return Orc.withSword();
  }
  return false
}

OrcRepository.prototype.add = function (orc) {
  this.orcs += 1
  if (orc.weapon == "sword") this.swords += 1
}

function Orc(name, weapon) {
  this.name = name
  this.weapon = weapon
}

Orc.withSword = function () {
  return new Orc(randomName(), "sword")
}

repo = new OrcRepository (1, 1)
orc = repo.getArmed() // => { name: "Zuul", weapon: "sword" }
repo.getArmed() // => false
repo.add(orc)
repo.getArmed() // => { name: "Zuul", weapon: "sword"}
```

While the `Orc` object itself might be a value object, the assignment needs to have a lifecycle, defining the start, the end, and the availability. We would need to get an orc from a repository of `Orc` objects, fulfilling the need to be able to guard the transport and return it as soon as the transport is done. In the preceding case, the `Orcs` repository is an entity, so we need to make sure that it is managed correctly otherwise we might end up with incorrect orc counts or unrecorded weapons, as both are bad for business. The orc in this case can be passed around freely, and we are isolated from its management.

More on entities

Entities come up regularly when building an application, and it is easy to fall into the trap of making most objects in the system entities, instead of value objects. The important thing to keep in mind is that value objects can perform a lot of work, and that dependencies on value objects are "cheap".

So why are dependencies on value objects "cheaper" than a dependency on an entity? When dealing with entities, we have to deal with state, so any modification being made can have an impact on other subsystems using this entity in their processing. The reason for this is the fact that each entity is a unique thing that can change, while a value object boils down to a collection of properties. When we pass around entities, we need to synchronize the consumers on the state of the entity, and possibly on all its dependent entities as well. This can get out of control very quickly. The following code shows complication when dealing with the interaction of multiple entities. We need to control multiple aspects when keeping the Wallet, inventory and the orc itself in a consistent state when adding and removing items:

```
function Wallet(coins) {
  this.money = coins
}

Wallet.prototype.pay = function (coin) {
  for(var i = 0; i < this.money.length; i++) {
    if (this.money[i].equals(coin) {
      this.money.splice(i, 1)
      return true
    }
  }
  return false
}

function Orc(wallet) {
  this.wallet = wallet
```

```
    this.inventory = []
  }

  Orc.prototype.buy = function (thing, price) {
    var priceToPay = new Coin(price)
    if (this.wallet.pay(priceToPay)) {
      this.inventory.unshift(thing)
      return true
    }
    return false
  }
```

In this case, we need to make sure that the buy action is not interrupted because a strange behavior could occur depending on other implementations. This would get even worse if the inventory had more behavior associated with it, such as a size check, then we would need to coordinate the two checks while making sure we can roll back without being interrupted. We have seen before how events can cause us a lot of problems here and this gets unwieldy fast. Even though it is of course unavoidable to deal with this at some level, being aware of the problems is important.

Entities need to have their lifecycle controlled in a way that makes sure there is no inconsistent state present. This makes handling entities more complicated and can also have an impact performance on due to locking and transaction control.

Managing the application's lifecycle

Entities and aggregations are all about managing this cycle at every level of the application. We can think about the application itself being the aggregation wrapped around all its components to manage the attached value objects and contained entities. At the level of our prisoner transfer, we treat the transfer itself as a transaction wrapping all the local dependents, and managing the eventual result of either a successful transfer or a failed one.

It is always possible to push the lifecycle management further up or down the chain of objects, and finding the right level can be hard. In the previous example, the assignment might as well be a value object managed by an aggregate up the chain to ensure its constraints are satisfied. The right level of abstraction at this stage is a decision that the developers of the system have to make. Pushing the transaction control too high and then making the transaction span more objects can be costly as the locks are more coarse and therefore concurrent operations are hindered; pushing it too low can result in a complex interaction between the aggregates.

Deciding the right level of abstraction to manage the lifecycle has a deeper influence into the application than is visible at first. Since entities are managed by their ID while being mutable, this means they are objects that need to be synchronized when dealing with concurrency, and because of this it influences the concurrency of the system as a whole.

Aggregations

Object orientation relies heavily on combining the functionality of multiple collaborators to achieve certain functionality. When building systems, there is often the problem that certain objects attract more and more functionality, and in that, becoming a kind of god object that is involved in almost every interaction in the system. The way around this is to let multiple objects collaborate to achieve the same functionality, but as a sum of small parts instead of one large object.

Building up those interconnected subsystems has a different problem, in that it tends to expose large and complex interfaces as the user needs to know more about the internals to use the system as the objects structure is being build up. Letting a client handle the internals of a subsystem is not a good way to model such a system, and this is where the concept of aggregation comes into play.

An aggregation allows use to expose one consistent interface to our clients and let them deal only with the parts they need to provide to make the system function as a whole, and let the outside entry point handle the different internal parts. In the previous chapter, *Chapter 4, Modelling the Actors*, we talked about aggregation in the example of a horse carriage being made up of all the elements needed to make it work as a whole. The same concept applies to other levels as well, and each subsystem we build is a kind of aggregation of its parts, comprising of entities and value objects along the way.

Grouping and interfaces

The questions we need to ask ourselves as developers are, at that point during our development, how do we group parts, where are the interfaces governing those aggregations best built, and what should they look like? Even though there is, of course, no strict formula for this, there are parts described in the following that can be used as guidance.

Interfaces should only require a client to provide the parts it actually cares about as being flexible, which often means that there are multiple entry points to a subsystem and clients touching a system through different points might step on others' toes along the way. We can borrow some classic techniques at this point and provide so-called `factory` methods to give us the entry point to the object graph that we need. This allows use to create an easily readable syntax instead of trying to take advantage of all the dynamic ways of to make the object creation flexible and accept very different parameters to provide the same functionality. The following code shows this kind of factory in the context of creating an orc. We want to have the object constructor as flexible as possible, while providing factory methods for the common case:

```
var AVAILABLE_WEAPONS = [ "axe", "axe", "sword" ]
var NAMES = [ "Ghazat", "Waruk", "Zaraugug", "Smaghed", "Snugug",
              "Quugug", "Torug", "Zulgha", "Guthug", "Xnath" ]

function Orc(weapon, rank, name) {
  this.weapon = weapon
  this.rank = rank
  this.name = name
}

Orc.anonymusArmedGrunt = function () {
  var randomName = NAMES[Math.floor(Math.random() * NAMES.length)]
  var weapon = AVAILABLE_WEAPONS.pop()
  return new Orc(weapon, "grunt", randomName)
}
```

In this example, we could have detected missing attributes and reshuffled the input parameters to ensure that generating an orc works with every kind of combination, but this quickly becomes unwieldy. As soon as the collaborators are no longer just simple strings like picked here for simplicity, we need to interact with more objects and control more interaction. By providing a factory function, we can express exactly what we intend to provide and don't need to resort to very complex handling.

Overall, the goal of grouping collaborators in aggregates and providing different interfaces for the access is to control the context, as well as to engrain the language of the domain more deeply in the project. Aggregates are there to provide a simpler view of the model data they aggregate to protect against inconsistent usage.

Services

For now, we have been expressing concepts around "things", but there are certain concepts that are best expressed around the act of doing something, and this is where services come in. Services are a first class element of domain-driven design, and their goal is to encapsulate actions in the domain that involves the coordination of many collaborators.

"[...]Verbs in Javaland are responsible for all the work, but as they are held in contempt by all, no Verb is ever permitted to wander about freely. If a Verb is to be seen in public at all, it must be escorted at all times by a Noun.

Of course "escort", being a Verb itself, is hardly allowed to run around naked; one must procure a VerbEscorter to facilitate the escorting. But what about "procure" and "facilitate?" As it happens, Facilitators and Procurers are both rather important Nouns whose job is is the chaperonment of the lowly Verbs "facilitate" and "procure", via Facilitation and Procurement, respectively.[...]"

- Steve Yegge - Thursday, March 30, 2006 - Execution in the Kingdom of Nouns

Services are a very useful but also often abused concept, and they come down to naming in general. The act of doing something can either be expressed in terms of a "thing" doing or naming the "doinger". For example, we could have a `Letter` and call the `send` method on it, letting it decided what to do and passing it the collaborators needed, for example:

```
function Letter(title, text, to) {
   this.title = title
   this.text = text
   this.to = to
}

Letter.prototype.send = function(postman) {
   postman.deliver(this)
}
```

The alternative is to have a service that handles the sending of the letter and calls it in a stateless way, passing all the collaborators to the service upon construction:

```
function LetterSender(postman, letter) {
   this.postman = postman
   this.letter = letter
}
```

```
LetterSender.prototype.send = function() {
  var address = this.letter.to
  postman.deliver(letter, address)
}
```

In a simple example, it is very obvious that the second approach seems complicated and does not add to the domain language of sending letters in any meaningful way. In more complex code, this is often overlooked because the complexity of a certain action needs to live somewhere. Which approach to choose comes down to the amount of functionality that can be encapsulated in the service. When a service exists only to split out a piece of code into a now separate but kind of homeless piece, a service is probably a bad idea. If we are able to encapsulate domain knowledge in the service, then we will have a valid reason to create one.

Having one object being named after what it does and having only one method in it which is actually the action should raise a red flag for any object-oriented programmer. Good services add to the domain and express a concept that has a solid foundation in the domain itself. This means there are names to express this concept. Services can encapsulate those concepts not directly backed by "things", and they should be named according to the domain.

Associations

In the previous section, we saw that the delivery of a letter is dependent on a postman. There is a certain relationship between the letter and the person who delivers it, but depending on the domain, this relationship might not be a very strong or relevant one. It could be relevant for our dungeon master to know who delivered which letter, for example, in case every deliveryman is instantly imprisoned and held responsible for the content of the post he or she delivers.

The ways of the orcs might not be as understandable as the rules of business often are. In this case, we would want to make sure that we put a label on each letter and the postman who delivered it, associating the letter with a certain person. The other way around is not relevant. As we model this in our domain, we want to carry this important knowledge across and have a way to associate the message in the process of delivery with the appropriate deliveryman. In code this can be done more easily; we might for example create a history for the letter, where each collaborator being associated with the delivery is linked.

The concept of associations between domain models is an integral part of the domain design, as most objects of whatever form will not work in complete independence. We want to codify as much knowledge as possible in the associations. When we think about associations between objects, the association itself can hold domain knowledge that we want to have incorporated in our model.

Insight during implementation

The concept of patterns is well established across object-oriented languages as well as other types. Many books have been written on it, and many discussions have been had that deal with encoding the knowledge of many developers in patterns to be used in enterprise, as well as other kinds of software. In the end, it comes down to using the right pattern at the right point during development, which is not only true for domain patterns but other software patterns as well.

In his book *Patterns of Enterprise Application Architecture*, Martin Fowler not only discusses the available options to deal with communication to a database by means of a `DataMapper` plugin plus domain layer, Transaction Scripts, Active Record, and so on, but also discusses when to use them. As with most things, the conclusion in the end is so that all choices have good and bad sides to them.

When working on software, there are multiple insights to gain as we move forward. A very valuable insight is the introduction of a new concept that was not clear before. To reach such a point there is no obvious way, what we can do is to start classifying the patterns we currently have in the software and making them as clear as possible to make the discovery of new concepts more likely. With a set of well separated pieces, discovering missing pieces if more likely to happen. When we are thinking about domain patterns, especially the various ways that we can classify certain elements of the application, the ways to classify are not always as clear as we would like them to be.

Recognizing domain patterns

As you saw in the example of handling sending the letter, we noticed that even though the proposed option uses a service to handle the collaboration, there are other ways to go about this. The problem with small examples like we have in this book is that it is hard to convey when a certain option has a benefit or when a certain design is overkill in the general context; this is especially true for complex architecture as domain-driven design is, after all if the application is done in a couple hundred lines of code, many problems the domain-driven design solves are not present.

When we write the code for a certain feature, we always need to be aware of the fact that the design of the components is not set in stone. An application might start out with a lot of entities being present, handling most interactions inline, as the system has not evolved enough yet to have a clear view on which interactions are complex and important enough to have them as a domain concept. Also, often the fact that we *use* the software means we recognize certain concepts, and by use as developers, I mean touching the interfaces and extending the software as a whole.

Not everything is an entity

Often, in domain-driven design it is easy to create entities for everything. The idea of an entity is a very common one in the mind of developers. Objects always have a fixed identity when we think about them as things in memory, and most languages by default compare this way, for example:

```
Function Thing(name) {
   this.name = name
}

aThing = new Thing("foo")
bThing = new Thing("foo")

aThing === bThing // => false
```

This makes it easy to just expect everything to be an entity, with its ID being whatever JavaScript considers it to be.

When we think about the domain, this of course does not always make sense, and we quickly start to recognize that certain things are not identified this way, which often moves certain parts of the application towards the use of value objects, for example.

Starting out as simple as possible is a good thing, but what makes the project a great place to work on over time is taking as many opportunities as possible to make things better. Even if the route does not end up being the one taken, the mere act of trying it makes the code better.

The **primitive obsession** anti-pattern is a trap often fallen into when not refactoring early and often. The problem is that new objects are introduced rarely and many concepts are represented by primitives, like an email as a string, or money values as pure integers. The problem is that the primitives don't encapsulate all the knowledge but just the pure property, and this leads to duplication of knowledge all over the place where a named concept such as an e-mail or a money object could have been shared.

Refactoring all the time towards malleable code

When we start to work toward letting the code guide our design in different ways, we notice the places that are continually changing, and the ones that trouble us with most new features, or even refactoring being implemented. Those are the pain points that we need to address.

In object-oriented programming, the single responsibility principle states that every class should have responsibility over a single part of the functionality provided by the software, and that responsibility should be entirely encapsulated by the class. All its services should be narrowly aligned with that responsibility

– the Single Responsibility Principle according to Wikipedia, originally defined by Robert C. Martin

We want our changes to be localized, and exploring a different route for the implementation of a certain feature should touch the least amount of code possible. This is the purpose of the **Single Responsibility Principle**, as defined by Robert C. Martin, which defines a responsibility as a reason to change. Together with the **Open/ closed principle**, making code open for extension but closed for modification, this leads to code being easy to work with due to known seams and building blocks.

The goal of domain-driven design is to take the concepts of object-oriented programming and take them to a higher level, so most concepts of object orientation apply to domain-driven design, as well. Whereas in object orientation we want to encapsulate objects, in domain driven design we encapsulate domain knowledge. We want each subsystem and each element of our domain to be as independent as possible and if we achieve this, the code will be easy to change along the way.

Implementing language guidance

Domain-driven design is all about encapsulating domain knowledge and the guiding force to contain and distribute knowledge is language. We have talked before about the fact that one of the goals of domain-driven design is to create a ubiquitous language in the project that is shared between the developers and the project owners or stakeholders to guide the implementation. And it has been hinted before that this is, of course, not a one way street.

As domain concepts are uncovered, it is often useful to establish and name the new concepts as a team to make them the established way of communication. Sometimes, these new names and meanings can make it back into the business, they will start to get used to describe the now named pattern and over a long time can make it back in the common language used in the domain cross businesses if they are considered useful.

In the original book on domain-driven design, by Eric Evans, he discusses the development of a financial software and how terms established made it back all the way to the Sales and Marketing departments to describe the new features of the software. Even though this might not be the case with your new additions to the business language, if an addition is helpful, at least core parts of the business will adopt them.

Working with and on the business language

Building a language of the domain is very different, depending on the domain. Very few domains already have a very specific language associated with them. If we look into accounting, for example, there are books written about what everything is called and how things interact. Similar things can also exist for established businesses, and even if there might not be a book to read up on it, following a person who does the business on a day-to-day basis can quickly reveal some concepts.

 Shadowing the process you are tasked to implement for a day can provide some very important insights. It can also hint in the areas where the business behaves in very specific way, those little things we as programmers otherwise come up against after the fact. Things that we see as illogical have a hard time fitting into our model.

Not many areas of business are this lucky, and especially in the world of young businesses developing new ideas, there is inherently a lack of established language. Also those businesses are most often the ones that invest heavily in a JavaScript-based application, so how can we deal with this?

Going back to the orc dungeon, we are dealing with a world that is very alien to us and that does not have a very established language to deal with its processes, as so far there was hardly ever a need for it. We dealt with this problem in the book already, as many terms are heavily overloaded in context. A notification could be a message to an orc to inform him that he is assigned to a certain prisoner transport, or a message to another dungeon to inform them of prisoners arriving, or a prison requesting new prisoners. How can we deal with situation?

Let's take the example of the orc master explaining to us how he would need to notify another dungeon:

Developer: What do you need when the dungeon is overflowing with prisoners?

Orc master: No problem! Let Xaguk deal with it?

Developer: As I know, Xaguk is the leader of the dungeon up north, so I guess you need to get a transport ready?

Orc master: Yes, I need to message Baronk to set up a transport and Xaguk for him to be ready.

He writes down two letters and calls for his goblin helper.

Orc master: Get this to Baronk, and this to Xaguk!

The goblin starts to run off, but just before he leaves the room through the south door, the master starts screaming.

Orc master: What are you doing? You need to get a raven and send this to Xaguk first!

The goblin looks very confused but starts running of the other way now.

Orc master: This happens all the time—the goblin just can't remember who is who, and he doesn't have to, but he needs to get the letters to the right office.

Developer: Ahh, so if you want to send a message to the other dungeon, you get a raven? When you message somebody insight the dungeon, it gets carried locally?

Orc master: That is right!

Developer: Okay, so we don't get confused in the system, I'm just going to call the messaging of another dungeon, to "raven" somebody, and locally we just continue calling it "message." Does this make sense?

Orc master: Yes! Hopefully the goblin will no longer mess up this way, as this has caused some strange conversations already.

This is a major simplification of how things like this could evolve, but the important thing that we as developers should take in pieces of the language that the business provides and incorporate them in the domain. This not only makes our life easier, but also improves business communication in general.

One thing to note is that we need to make sure we don't force our very specific language into the business, that is, if a certain concept does not get adopted, be ready to scrap it. After all, the only thing worse than an unnamed concept is a confusingly named concept. Building a language needs to come from the domain, and should not be forced on the domain. A name that does not stick is either one that names an unimportant concept, or one that is not descriptive enough to stick.

If an unimportant concept is named, it often forces unnecessary attention to it, and this can cause trouble down the road as we might be reluctant to change it or to adapt to new needs when we consider it too important. Consider, for example, that we developed the concept of automatic prisoner cell assignment, which uses an algorithm to determine the optimal cell for the amount of prisoners we have. This seemed very important as we want the dungeon to be used as optimally as possible. One day, a single new prisoner arrives and the system starts the calculation determining the optimal cell for him, while the guard is saying, "Why is this taking so long? Every time! I already know where I put him, I just cram him in cell number 1!" This is valid user feedback—even though we might have found a way to optimally use the dungeon, this might not actually be important as the orc sees the amount of prisoners per cell in a far more relaxed way than we do. The concept of automatic assignment is something that never really caught on; we have never heard anybody talking about it, so we might as well remove the whole thing, making the system easier for us and the users.

Systems, of course, not only serve the users; they might also serve other systems along the way. So keeping in mind who is the actually user can have a major influence on decisions.

Building context

We have been talking a lot about the language we use, and how systems interact and what they are comprised of, but there is a higher level we need to touch as well: *How do systems interact with other systems?*

In the server world, there is currently a strong focus on microservices and their building and interaction. The important takeaway is that having a system that a small team owns is easier to maintain than a system built by a larger team; this is only half the story, so services need to interact after all. Microservices are the more technical approach to the domain-driven design bounded context.

The following diagram shows how an interaction in a microservice world can take place. We have a lot of small services calling each other to accomplish a bigger task:

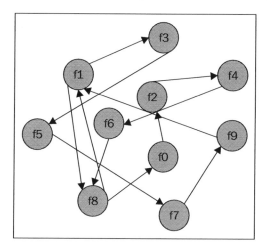

Interaction not only happens on the API level but at the developer level, as well.

Separation and shared knowledge

Teams working on different parts of the application need to be aware of how they are able to share knowledge and work together when change arises. Eric Evans devotes a large section of domain-driven design to the patterns we see in practice. We see patterns a lot in software development, be it software patterns such as `DataMapper`, `ActiveRecord`, or the patterns Eric Evans discusses that are about the process of working together.

In the current world of microservices, we seem to have moved away from deep integration towards a more flexible way of touching other parts of the system only very lightly. It is still important to share a domain across the team, and a map of what touches what is becoming more important than ever.

Summary

In this chapter, we have gone into a lot of detail on how to separate out systems and how to deal with concepts throughout the application, mostly on the smaller scale of a project, and how it interacts with the larger scale.

There are many ideas that have been used in other places we can draw from when building the project, be it object-oriented design or be it software architecture patterns; the important thing to keep in mind is that nothing should be set in stone. One very important thing about domain-driven design is that it constantly changes, and that this change is a good thing. As soon as a project becomes too solid, it becomes hard to change and this means the business using it can no longer evolve alongside its software, which ultimately means switching to another system and different software, or rewriting the existing software.

The next chapter will touch more on the higher level view of the intertwining pieces of the project as a whole, going into detail about the context that each part of the project is set in.

6
Context Map – The Big Picture

The dungeon manager application, for now, only contains the functionality to manage prisoner transportation, but as our application grows, the need to organize the code increases as well. The number of developers able to concurrently work on a piece of software is limited. Jeff Bezos (founder and CEO of Amazon.com) once stated that the size of a team should be no more than that can be fed by two pizzas (`http://www.wsj.com/news/articles/SB1000142405297020391430457662710299683 1200`). The idea is that any team larger than this will have trouble with communication as the number of connections within this team grows very quickly. As we add more people, the amount of communication needed to keep everybody up to date grows as well, and sooner or later the team will be slowed down by its constant need for meetings.

This fact causes somewhat of a dilemma because, as we described earlier, the perfect application would be one where everybody would know everything about how the development happened and how the decisions around the changes were made. This leaves us with very few options: we can either decide to not grow the team, building the application but opting for a slower development cycle that can be handled by this team alone (along with a smaller feature-set on the application as a whole), or alternatively we can try to make multiple teams work on the same application. Both strategies have been successful as far as business goes. Staying small and growing naturally, while most likely not resulting in hockey-stick growth can result in a well run and successful company as the likes of Basecamp Inc. and other independent software developers have proved. On the other hand, this does not work for applications that are inherently complex and aim for a much broader scope, so the likes of Amazon and Netflix, for example, started growing their teams around the idea of creating a larger application comprising of smaller parts.

Assuming that we opt for the idea of domain-driven design, we more likely have an application that is part of the inherently complex realm, so the following chapter will introduce some common ways to handle this scenario. One important point not to miss when designing an application like this is that we should always strive to reduce complexity as far as possible. You will learn:

- How to organize a growing application technically
- How to test the integration of applications in a system
- How to organize expanding contexts in the application

Don't fear the monolith

In recent times, there has been a strong move toward breaking applications apart and designing them as a set of services communicating via messages. This is a well-established concept for large-scale applications; the problem is finding the correct time to break the application apart and also deciding whether breaking it apart is the right thing to do. When we break an application into multiple services, we increase the complexity at this point since we now have to deal with handling communication problems crossing multiple services. We have to consider the resilience of the services, and the dependencies each service has, to provide its features.

On the other hand, when we break an application apart at a late stage, problems arise when extracting logic from the application. There is no reason why a monolith application can't be well-factored and remain easy to maintain for a long time. Breaking up an application will always cause problems, and staying with a well-factored application for a long time works. The problem is that a large codebase with a lot of developers working on it is more likely to deteriorate.

How can we avoid such problems? The best way is to design the application in a way that breaks it up as simply as possible but keeps the problem of communication between sub-systems out of the picture for as long as possible. This is what a strong domain model excels at; the domain will allow us to have strong separation from the underlying frameworks, but also makes it clear where to break apart the application when we have to.

In the domain model, we already established areas that can be separated out later because we designed them as separate parts. A good example is the prisoner transport, which is hidden behind an interface that can later be extracted. There can be a team working on just the prisoner transport feature, and as long as there is no change to the public interface exposed, their work can be done without worrying about other changes.

Going a step further, it does not matter where the actual logic is executed, from a purely logical perspective. The prisoner transfer might just be a façade that calls into a separate backend, or it might be run in a process. This is what a well-factored application is all about—it provides an interface sub-domain functionality and exposes it in an abstract enough way to make the underlying system easy to change.

We only want to separate out a service if it is necessary, and if there is a clear benefit in doing so, reducing the complexity of deployment or development dependencies so the development of the process can be scaled, at best, along with a team to take care of the service moving forward.

Service-oriented architecture and microservices

In the extreme form, a **service-oriented architecture (SOA)** ends in microservices; a concept where each service is only responsible for a very limited feature set, therefore with very few reasons to change and is easy to maintain. In terms of domain-driven design, this means that a service is established for each bounded context inside the application. The context can eventually be broken down to mean that each aggregate is managed by separate services. The service managing the aggregate can ensure the inner consistency, and the interface as a service means that the access points are very clearly defined. Most of the problems are shifted to the communication layer, which has to deal with the resilience. This can be a big challenge to the communication layer in the application, and also for the services themselves that now have to deal with more failure modes due to the communication failing between the dependents. Microservices have been used in some scenarios with great success, but the overall concept is still young and needs to prove itself in a wider range of use cases.

The micro-service architecture is more or less an extension of the actor model, only if the move to making the actors self-sufficient services is an extension to this. This increases the communication overhead for better isolation; in domain-driven design, this could mean constructing services around entities, as they are the managers around the life cycle of parts of the application.

Overall, whatever architecture ends up being the one of choice, it is useful to think about how to prepare the application for being broken up later. Carefully crafting a flexible domain model and leveraging bounded contexts is the key to evolving application design in such a way. Even in the case where the application is never actually broken into pieces, having a clear separation makes each part easier to work with and the combined application less error-prone because of better understandable, and therefore simpler to modify, components.

A key point there is to have the core domain well identified and it is best to have it isolated to evolve it from other pieces of the system. Not every piece of the software is always going to be well designed, but having a core domain and its sub-domains isolated and defined makes the application as a whole ready to evolve, as those are the core pieces of the application.

Keeping it all in your head

Every time we open our editor of choice to work on code, there is a bit of overhead to know where to start and what section we actually need to modify. Understanding where to start a modification to move toward a certain goal is often the difference between an application that is a joy to work on and one nobody likes to touch.

When we start working on a piece of code, there is a maximum amount of context we can keep in our head any a given time. Even though it is not possible to give exact constraints, it is easy to notice when a certain part of the code exceeds this limit. It is often the point where refactoring gets harder, the test starts to become brittle, and unit tests seem to lose their value as their passing no longer ensures the functionality of the system. In the open source world, this is often a breaking point for a project and it is very visible due to its open nature. Either a library or application at this point proves valuable enough if people invest their time into really understanding the inner workings and continue to work towards making progress toward a more modular design, or the development stops. Enterprise applications suffer from the same fate, except that people are much more hesitant to give up on a project that provides a source of income or another important business aspect.

When projects become complicated, often people fear any modifications and nobody really understands what is going on anymore. When the pain and the uncertainty starts to grow, it is important to recognize this and start to separate the contexts of the application to keep its size manageable.

Recognizing the contexts

As we have drawn out the application, we have been recognizing certain parts of the application and the way they communicate with each other. We can use this knowledge now to make sure we have an idea of what the context of the application could look like:

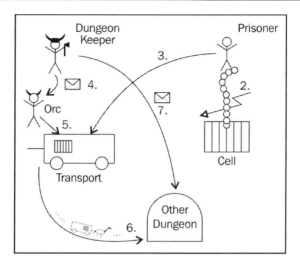

In *Chapter 1, A Typical JavaScript Project*, we had about six contexts in the realm with which we were dealing. With the understanding gained from recent chapters, this has changed a bit, but the basics are there. Those contexts are identified as the communication between them happens by exchanging messages and not by modifying the internal state. In a case where we are building an API, we can't rely on the fact that we are in a situation where the internal state can be modified, nor should there be a way to reach inside a context and modify its internals, as this is a very deep coupling between contexts that would obviate the usefulness of contexts in general.

Messages are the key foundation of an easy-to-model API; if we think in messages, it is easy to image breaking apart the application and the messages no longer being sent locally, but over a network. Of course, breaking up an application is still not easy because suddenly there is a lot more complexity to deal with, but having the ability to deal with the messaging is a big part of the complexity out of the way already.

The functional programming language **Erlang** takes this concept as far as possible. Erlang makes it easy to split applications apart into so-called processes, which are only able to communicate via messages being sent. This allows Erlang to relocate the processes to different machines and abstract away a whole slew of problems of multiprocessor machines, or multimachine systems.

Having a well-defined API allows us to make refactoring changes inside the context without breaking the applications on the outside. The contexts become roles in our system that we can regard as black boxes, and we can model other parts with the knowledge they encapsulate abstracted out. Inside a context, an application is a coherent whole, and represents its data in an abstracted way to the outside. When we expose domains and sub-domains as interfaces, we generate the building blocks to a malleable system. When they need to share data, there is a clear way to do it, and the goal should always be to share underlying data and expose different views on this data.

Testing in contexts

As we identify the contexts we can regard as black boxes, we should start using this knowledge in our tests as well. We have already seen how mocking allows us to separate us based on different roles, and a context in this way is a perfect candidate for a role to mock during our unit testing. As we break our application into contexts, we can, of course, also start with different styles of testing in different contexts, making the development process evolve as our understanding and the application changes. When we do this, we need to keep in mind that the application as a whole needs to continue running, so the integration of the application needs to be tested as well.

Integration across boundaries

At the boundaries of contexts, there are multiple things we need to test from the view of the context developer:

1. Our side of the context needs to adhere to its contract, which means the API.

2. The integration of the two contexts needs to work, so cross-boundary tests need to be in place.

For the first point, we can think of our tests as the consumers of the API. When we think about our messaging API for example, we want to have a test confirming that our API does what it promises. This is best served by an outside-in test covering the contract on the side of the context. Have a fictive `Notifier` that works as follows, as we previously used the notifier sending a message via the `message` function:

```
function Notifier(backend) {
  this.backend = backend
}

function createMessageFromSubject(subject) {
  return {} // Not relevant for the example here.
}
```

```
Notifier.prototype.message = function (target, subject, cb) {
  var message = createMessageFromSubject(subject)
  backend.connectTo(target, function (err, connection) {
    connection.send(message)
    connection.close()
    cb()
  })
}
```

We need to test whether the backend is called in the correct way when the notifier is called with the public API:

```
var sinon = require("sinon")

var connection = {
  send: function (message) {
    // NOOP
  },
  close: function () {
    // NOOP
  }

}

var backend = {
  connectTo: function (target, cb) {
    cb(null, connection)
  }
}

describe("Notifier", function () {
  it("calls the backend and sends a message", function () {
    var backendMock = sinon.mock(backend)
    mock.expects("connectTo").once()

    var notifier = new Notifier(backendMock)
    var dungeon = {}
    var transport = {}
    notifier.message(dungeon, transport, function (err) {
      mock.verify()
    })
  })
})
```

This would not be an extensive test but the basic assertion is that the backend we are using, which the notifier abstracts us from, is called. To make this more valuable, we would also need to assert the correct way of calling, as well as the calling of the dependencies further down.

The second point requires an integration test to be set up to cover the interaction between the two or more contexts without the involvement of mocks or stubs. This of course means that the test will most likely be more complicated than a test allowing mocks and stubs to tightly control the environment, and therefore it is often limited to quite a simple test, to ensure that a basic interaction works. An integration test should not go into too much detail in this case, as this might ossify the API more than intended. The following code tests the integration of the prisoner transfer system in the system as a whole, using the different required subsystems like the dungeon as integration points:

```
var prisonerTransfer = require("../../lib/prisoner_transfer")
var dungeon = require("../../lib/dungeon")
var inmates = require("../../lib/inmates")
var messages = require("../../lib/messages")
var assert = require("assert")

describe("Prisoner transfer to other dungeons", function () {

  it("prisoner is moved to remote dungeon", function (done) {
    var prisoner = new inmates.Prisoner()
    var remoteDongeon = new dungeon.remoteDungeon()
    var localDungeon = new dungeon.localDungeon()
    localDungeon.imprison(prisoner)
    var channel = new messages.Channel(localDungeon, remoteDungeon)

    assert(localDungeon.hasPrioner(prisoner))
    prisonerTransfer(prisoner, localDungeon, remoteDungeon, channel,
function (err) {
        assert.ifError(err)
        assert(remoteDungeon.hasPrioner(prisoner))
        assert(!localDungeon.hasPrioner(prisoner))
        done()
    })
  })
})
```

The preceding code shows how much more involved an end-to-end test ensuring a prisoner transfer can be. Due to this complexity, it only makes sense to test simple interactions as otherwise the end-to-end tests quickly become hard to maintain with small changes, and they should only cover the interactions on a higher level.

The goal of end-to-end or, integration tests across the boundaries of the system, is to ensure that the basic interactions work. The goal of unit tests is that the module in itself behaves as we want it to. This leaves a level open, which becomes obvious when running a service in production.

TDD and testing in production

Test-driven development allows us to design a system that is easy to change and evolve; on the contrary, it does not ensure a perfect function of course. We first write a "broken" test, a test where the underlying functionality is still missing, and then write the code to satisfy it. We don't write tests to be perfectly safe from production bugs, because we can never anticipate all the possible complications that may arise. We write the tests to allow our system to be flexible and also to allow it to be ready for production in the sense that we can introspect its behavior and have the contexts reasonably well isolated to deal with failure.

When moving code to production, we are exercising the system in a new way, and for this we need to be ready to monitor and introspect. This kind of introspection and monitoring also allows easy tests due to the injection of logging modules and others that allow simpler assertions of integration tests.

We have now seen how a system of contexts can help us create a more stable and easier to maintain system. In the following section, we are focusing on how to actually maintain the context within the application to fight the leaking of abstractions and leaking context across, and how this relates to different ways of organizing the application.

The different ways to manage contexts

So far, the main purpose of the context in our application has been to separate different modules and make the complexity of the whole application more manageable by abstracting out APIs. The other important benefits of separate contexts are the fact that we can start to explore different ways of managing application development in those decoupled parts.

The way applications are developed evolves as the industry around software evolves at a rapid pace. Development principles that were state of the art just a couple years ago are being frowned upon now and developers want to move to new ways of making them more productive while promising bug-free, easier to manage applications. Of course, switching out the development principles is not free, and more often than not new ways don't necessarily match the way complete organizations can, or want, to work. By separating out the contexts of the application, we can start exploring those new ways alongside the well-established ones and keep the team evolving and developing alongside the applications they maintain.

The first step towards manageable contexts is drawing a map of their relationships and starting to make a clear separation, using the language we established. With this map, we can start to think of ways to divide the application and break it into different ways to enable maximum productivity within the team.

Drawing a context map

The prisoner transport application that we have been following throughout the book so far involves multiple contexts. Each context can be abstracted by a clear API, and aggregates multiple collaborators to make the prisoner transport, as a whole, work. We can follow these collaborators in the integration test we have seen before, and draw out their relationship on a map for everybody on the project to keep in mind. The following diagram shows an outline of the different contexts involved in the prisoner transport, including their role:

```
┌─────────────────────────────────────────────────────────────────┐
│  Prisoner Transport Contexts                                      │
│                                                                   │
│  Prisoner Management : Inmates    │  Dungeon                      │
│  - Prisoner listing               │  - Top level Dungeon aggregate│
│  - Location assignment            │  - Orc Management             │
│  - checkin/checkout               │  - Material Management (Carriages, Weapons) │
│                                   │  - Message Hub (Local+Remote) │
│                                                                   │
│  Messaging System                 │  Transports                   │
│  - Channels                       │  - Transport Error Handling   │
│  - Delivery                       │  - Statistics                 │
│                                   │  - Initialization Automation  │
└─────────────────────────────────────────────────────────────────┘
```

The map, for now, involves four main contexts as we saw in the previous integration test:

- Prisoner management
- The dungeons
- The messaging system
- The transports

Each context is responsible for providing the collaborators needed to make an actual transport between the dungeons happen, and provided the API stays consistent, it can be replaced with a different implementation.

Investigation into the context shows differences that are going to increase as the application evolves, which means different strategies are needed to manage the contexts. There is the dungeon as the main entry point to the application, which manages most of the raw resources. The dungeon is going to be like the sun in the dungeon management solar system. It provides access to the resources, which can then be used to accomplish different tasks. Due to this, the dungeon is a shared core of the application.

On the other hand, there are different sub-domains that use the resources provided by the dungeon that gather around. The messaging system, for example, provides infrastructure to different systems, in a largely decoupled way to augment tasks as they are done by other systems. The prisoner transfer we have seen is one of the sub-domains tying those other sub-domains together. We use resources provided by the dungeon to build a prisoner transfer, and we use the decoupled messaging functionality to augment the transfer task.

Those three systems show how we have different contexts working together and providing resources to accomplish the tasks the system is to build. As we build them, we need to think about how those sub-domains should be related. Depending on the different types of subsystem that are being built, different forms of context relationships are useful and best support the development. One thing to keep in mind, so as long as the application is simple enough, is that most of those will add more overhead to the development than they add flexibility, as sharing aspects of the application will, by definition, become more complicated than it has been before.

The monolithic architecture

When starting out with development, the team developing the application is most likely small and the context of the application is in itself not large yet. At this stage, it most likely does not make sense to break out the contexts of the application domain, as those are still flexible and have not evolved enough to warrant a separate team to take care of them. Also, APIs at this stage are not stable enough to implement a solid abstraction, no matter how much planning has gone into the details beforehand.

Martin Fowler has been talking about this as well and he recommends a strategy of building a monolith first and breaking it up as needed. You can find more on this on his blog at http://martinfowler.com/bliki/MonolithFirst.html.

At this stage, application development will progress best using a monolithic architecture that provides shared access to the models. This does not mean, of course, that everything should be one big pile of code, but especially in a monolith it is easy to break out objects as everybody has access to them anyway. This will make it easier to break apart the application afterwards as borders tend to evolve during development.

This is also the way we have been developing the application so far; even though we recognize that there are contexts, those contexts don't necessarily mean separation into different applications or domains, but for now they are a map in the developer's mind to guide the location of the code as well as the flow of interactions. Taking a look at the prisoner transport, it can look like this:

```
prisonerTransfer = function (prisoner, otherDungeon, ourDungeon,
notifier, callback) {
  var keeper = ourDungeon.getOrc()
  var carriage = ourDungeon.getCarriage()
  var transfer = prepareTransfer(carriage, keeper, prisoner)
  if (transfer) {
    notifier.message(dungeon, transfer)
    callback()
  } else {
    callback(new Error("Transfer initiation failed."))
  }
}

function prepareTransfer(carriage, keeper, prisoner) {
  return {} // as a placeholder for now
}
```

Right now, the code accesses each part of the application directly. Even though the communication is wrapped into an object that controls the flow, the prisoner transfer has a lot of interaction happening, which will need to be accessed over the network if the application is broken apart. This kind of organization is typical for a monolithic application and will change when it is broken into different pieces, but the overall contexts will remain.

A shared kernel

We have already seen that the dungeon is like the sun in our orc dungeon management universe, so it only makes sense to share its functionality across the applications that interact with it in some way.

This kind of development is a **shared kernel**. The dungeon itself provides functionality that will need to be replicated in many different places unless it is shared in some way, and since the functionality is such a crucial part, it does not go well with a slow interface that is part of a supply chain, for example.

The dungeon provides many useful interfaces for the different parts that use it, so the functionality needs to be developed in tandem with the consumers. Going back to the prisoner transport, the code will look like this:

```
var PrisonerTransfer = function (prisoner, ourDungeon) {
  this.prisoner = prisoner
  this.ourDungeon = ourDungeon
  this.assignDungeonRessources()
}

PrisonerTransfer.prototype.assignDungeonRessources = function () {
  var resources = this.ourDungeon.getTransferResources()
  this.carriage = resources.getCarriage()
  this.keeper = resources.getKeeper()
}

PrisonerTransfer.prototype.prepare = function () {
  // Make the transfer preparations
  return true;
}

PrisonerTransfer.init = function (prisoner, otherDungeon,
ourDungeon, notifier, callback) {
  var transfer = new PrisonerTransfer(prisoner, ourDungeon)
  if (transfer.prepare()) {
    notifier.message(otherDungeon, transfer)
    callback()
  } else {
    callback(new Error("Transfer initiation failed."))
  }
}
```

In the preceding code, we used a common pattern, which uses an `init` method to encapsulate some logic needed to initialize the dungeon. This is often useful to make the creation easy to use from the outside, and instead of handling it in a complex constructor, we move it out to a separate factory method. The advantage is that the return of a simple method is easier to handle than using a complex constructor, as a failing constructor might end in a half-initialized object.

The important point in this is that the dungeon now supports a specific endpoint to provide the resources needed for the transfer to happen. This would most likely lock the given resources and initialize a transaction for them so they don't get reused without their reuse being possible in the physical world.

Due to our shared kernel nature, this change can happen in the prisoner transfer and the dungeon part of the application in tandem. The shared kernel is, of course, not without problems, as it creates strong coupling between the parts. It is always useful to keep this in mind and think twice about whether pieces are really needed in the shared kernel or whether they belong in another part of the application. Shared data does not mean there is a reason to share code. The view of what a prisoner transfer is can be different throughout the application: while the transfer itself might care more about details, the messaging service sharing the data of the transfer to create a message to send cares only about the target and the source, as well as the prisoners involved in the transfer. So sharing code between the two contexts would confuse each domain with unnecessary and unrelated knowledge.

The architecture of a shared context like this means that the teams working inside the shared context must work closely together, and that this part of the application has to be vigorously refactored and reviewed so it does not get out of hand. It is a straight evolution of the monolith, so to speak, but it takes the application a step further towards being split into multiple ones.

For many applications, splitting out some basic elements with a lot of churn is enough, and the application can evolve much more quickly using a shared kernel where the development team coordinates. This of course forces the team to trust each others decisions in general and the communication overhead between the engineers can grow with the shared kernel, evolving at this point, the application has solidified to a stage where teams can take over the responsibilities for application parts, rolling them in their own.

The APIs

Building distinct applications requires a set of APIs that can be relied upon. With APIs like this, it is possible to extract certain sub-domains from the main domain and application, which can start to evolve completely separately to the main application as long as they continue to conform to the same API as before.

It is important to identify a sub-domain first to allow it to have a clean API layer to build upon. Looking at the context map will show the interactions of the sub-domains, and those interactions are what an API model should be based on. Starting out by building in a more monolithic way and breaking out pieces as they are solidified in their sub-domain will lead towards this naturally.

Conforming to the same API as before is often only regarded as taking the same input and producing the same output, there is more to it so to provide a drop-in replacement. New applications need to provide similar guarantees towards response time and other service levels, such as data persistence for example. A drop-in replacement is easier said than done in most cases, but evolving an application toward better service levels is often easier in isolation.

As we develop the application, we are now free to branch off while staying true to the mission of the application. We are providing a service to other applications who need to conform to our way of doing things but only up to the call of the application.

The customer and the supplier

An application that provides a service is a supplier of a certain service. We can think of the messaging system as such a service. It provides other applications with an entry point to send messages across certain end points. Those end points need to provide the necessary calls if they want to receive messages while the messaging system takes care of the delivery of the message. An application using the messaging system needs to call into the system in a certain way.

Such a way of interaction is very abstract, and a good application like this does not provide many endpoints but very high-level entry points to the system in general to make the use as easy as possible.

Developing a client

Using an internal application like this can be done in multiple ways. The interface can be very simple, for example, a very basic call over HTTP like this:

```
$ curl -X POST --date ' {"receiver":1,"sender":2,"message":"new
transfer of one prisoner"'  http://api.messaging.orc
```

A call like this does not need a separate client for most languages as it is very easy to interact with and will be bundled in to the customer application in whatever way is deemed best.

Not every application can provide such an easy interface of course, so at this stage there is the need to provide a client, which at best is shared between the different customers of the application, to not duplicate work. This can be provided either by the developing application in the case of complex clients or can be initiated by one of the customer applications and then shared in the same style as a shared kernel. While in most bigger systems it seems that the client is more often than not provided by the application development team, this is not necessarily the best way as they are not always aware of the intricacies that using their application involves, and therefore invite wrapping clients for each consumer to evolve alongside the internal client.

The conformist

The split of an application into an API supplier and consumer is a very distinct split and, even with the provided clients, it means that the application now consists of multiple parts that are no longer developed as a unit. This kind of split is often suggested to increase the speed of development as the team can be smaller and there is no longer such a strong communication needed. However, this comes at a price when the two separate applications need to work together to provide new features.

When we need to communicate across borders, it is expensive, not only in terms of networking and method call speed, but in terms of team communication overall. The teams providing different parts of the application are not set up to work with each other and the time it takes to set this structure up is an overhead we have to pay for every time a feature is developed in collaboration.

> *Organizations which design systems ... are constrained to produce designs which are copies of the communication structures of these organizations…*
>
> *- M. Conway*

This kind of development is kind of the inverse effect of *Conway's law*, because as organizations will produce systems constrained by their structure, forcing different structures will inadvertently slow down the team as it is not fit to develop such an application.

When confronted with an increasing application, we need to make a choice: we can either decide to break up the application or deal with the result of growing pains. Dealing with the pains of a legacy application and just conforming to the development route it took can be a good choice depending on where the overall system is supposed to go. If, for example, the application is in maintenance mode for some time and it is unlikely that it will gain features any time soon, deciding to just continue on this route, even if the model is not perfect and the code base seems legacy, might well be the best choice.

Being a conformist is the unpopular choice, but it follows the suit of "never do a rewrite" and, after all, it is more rewarding to work on an application that is actually useful than on one that might be nicely engineered but does not provide value and is therefore neglected sooner or later.

The anticorruption layer

There is a certain point in the application's life where just adding more features and conforming to the already present design is not productive anymore. At this stage, it makes sense to split from the main application and start to break out of the cycle of ever increasing complexity in the software. At this stage, it is a good idea to reform the domain language as well and see where the legacy codebase fits into the model, as this allows you to create solid abstractions and design a nice API on top of it. This kind of development provides a façade over the code, and by this, we mean providing a layer to shield the application from old terms and problems that might leak in.

 The anticorruption layer is a very important pattern when it comes to improving applications that are already in production. Isolating a new feature makes it easier not only to test , but also can increase reliability and ease the introduction of new patterns.

Isolating the methodologies

As we build a layer like this, we are all about isolating us from the underlying technology; this of course means that we should also isolate ourselves from the ways of building software present below, and we can start using all the new ways developed since the original application was started.

This has one very bad side-effect, which is that the old application instantly becomes the legacy not many people want to work on anymore and much blame might be thrown toward it. Make sure such a strong split is necessary for this reason.

An anticorruption layer might also make sense in the case where an outside application is integrated into the system, for example, credit card processing by an outside banking system. External dependencies are best served when isolated from the core application, and be it just for the fact that the external API can change and adjusting all callers is most likely more complicated then adjusting the internal abstraction. This is exactly what an anticorruption layer is good at, so soon your internal dependencies are best treated like external ones.

Separate ways

Similar to an anticorruption layer, in a more separate way, tries to solve the problem of an application growing apart in the domain. As we develop a common language across the system and are breaking the application apart, the language will become more refined for some models and the models will increase in complexity in certain applications, but not necessarily in others. This can lead to problems where a shared core is used because this core needs to incorporate the maximum complexity required by each sub-domain and therefore continues to grow while we would rather keep it small.

The problem is deciding when a certain application needs to be split at the domain model level because the increased complexity for one part does not enhance another parts' usability anymore. In our application, the likely candidate is the dungeon model that is shared across the other applications. We want to keep it as small as possible, but parts of the application will have different demands on it. The messaging subsystem will have to focus on the delivery of messages to the dungeon and increase the complexity of this part, while the system to handle prisoner transport prerequisites will care about other resource management parts.

Unrelated applications

With different applications having such different requirements towards the core domain, it can make sense not share the model but build a specific one for the applications that need it, sharing only a datastore or some other means to share the state. The goal is to reduce dependencies and this can mean only sharing what actually needs to be shared, even if the names might suggest otherwise. When sharing a data store, it is important to keep in mind that only the sub-domain that owns the data should be able to modify it, while all others should be using an API to access the data, or only have read-only access. It comes down to whether the overhead of an API is sustainable, or whether direct integration is needed for performance.

When applications start using models in different ways and the only reason they share a model is the fact that the model is named the same, we can start to look for more specific names that are fit for purpose, and at some point we can even get rid of the primary model completely. In our dungeon example, the case may be that, over time, the dungeon itself gets reduced to only being the entry point of the application, acting as a router to the managing sub-domain applications.

Moving more functionality outside the initially shared context of the application into other contexts means that we reduce the surface of our shared sub-domain, and that we misidentified the role of this domain in the beginning. This is nothing bad since every application should be built to evolve, and as contexts become more clear, this can in turn clarify the sub-domain borders that were previously unclear.

 Don't get too attached to your understanding of the borders of domains and sub-domains. As gaining experience from business experts can improve your understanding of a sub-domain, so can the refining of a bounded context in turn influence the domain.

An open protocol

The last step in making applications truly independent is publishing them as an open protocol. The point is to make the core functionality of the application accessible openly from the outside as a published standard. This is very seldom the case as it requires a lot of maintenance and setup initially. The best candidates for an open protocol are special communication layers used to communicate with the application to allow external clients.

The API of an application can be considered an open protocol when it invites in external users, and maybe even external clients. In our dungeon applications we might, at some point, want to make the messaging subsystem an open protocol to allow other dungeons to plug in via their own local applications, and therefore establishing the standard in the Dungeon Management™.

As this stage, when thinking about the Open Protocols, what we need to focus on is the fact of how we can share knowledge of the protocol in an effective way.

Sharing knowledge

We split the application apart into multiple sub-applications of the sub-domains, we do this to increase the size of the team and enable better cooperation between them. This also means that the team needs to find a way to share the information about the application and their usage with new developers as well as with developers tapping into the sub-domain to accomplish a certain goal.

The domain language is an important part of our design and we invested some time into building it throughout the development so far. We can draw on this and make this language available for other developers. The language, as we have seen it, slightly adjusts for each module and is a working document that needs to be kept up to date, and that means we need to find a way to keep it published.

The publishing language

The language we have been developing is an ever-evolving document, and as such we have to think about how to share the knowledge embedded in it. Again let's first define what we would do in a perfect world and see how we can approximate this situation.

In a perfect world, the team that started out developing the application would stay together for the whole lifetime of the application and continue to grow, but the core developers would always be there. A team like this would have the major advantage of the terminology and the assumptions of the project being shared by the team as they have been following the application through its life, and new developers would join and learn from the core team by osmosis, so to speak. They would slowly adapt to the team and follow the rules, breaking them if necessary, and if agreed upon via the consensus of the team.

We don't live in a perfect world though, and teams are likely to have some churn where core developers leave for whatever reason and are replaced with new faces. When this happens, there is the risk that the core principles of the application can could be lost, that the language around the project does not follow the original rules more, and many other bad things. Luckily, compared to olden times, we don't have to rely on word of mouth but can document our findings for others to find.

Creating the documentation

Documentation is often not the favorite part of software development, but this comes from the fact that a lot of documentation is not useful in many projects. When we create documentation, the important thing is to not state the obvious but to actually document the problems and ideas arising during development.

Often, the documentation found on projects is the outline of the methods, what parameters they take in, and what they return. This is a good start but not not the end of all documentation necessary. When different people are using the project they need to understand the intention behind it to use the API properly. When we create an application and decide on what kind of features we want and how they work, this is important to document. So far in this book, we have been focusing a lot on how to think about application development and also how to make sure it is in an understandable form for others to follow. All this is documentation that needs to be kept around. We want to be sure that the next person can follow the thinking that went into the development, knows what the terms mean, and how they relate to each other.

A good way to start is to keep a central document where this kind of information lives close to the application and is accessible to everybody interested. Making the document as short as possible and having a way to see it evolve along with the project is key, so having some kind of versioning is a very useful feature. Going back in time in source code is very common to find out how a certain piece of code has changed, and being able to relate the right piece of documentation to it is very helpful.

 Keeping a simple text file as the README for the project is a good place to start. This README can live inside the application repository, making the relationship between documentation and application a very strong one.

In the following we see this by the example of the canned fake API server, available at `https://github.com/sideshowcoder/canned`:

The important points for documentation are:

- The goal of the project in a short statement
- The design ideas followed throughout the project to guide new developers
- Example usages of features
- Implementation notes for very important pieces of code
- The change history of major changes
- The setup instructions

Updating the documentation

Keeping the documentation close to the application has some essential advantages; it is just way too easy to neglect some document off in a wiki somewhere that needs special permissions to access, while looking at something every day when working on a project will more likely be kept up-to-date.

Documentation is a living and breathing piece of the overall project and it therefore needs to be part of the project itself. Especially in the modern, open source inspired development world, the idea that everybody should be able to contribute to a project quickly is ingrained in the developer culture and this is a good thing. Code speaks louder than a thousand architecture specs, so to speak, and therefore limiting the documentation to the core design ideas while letting the code explain the specific implementation makes the documentation more useful in the long run and keeps developers engaged in the updating process.

Tests are not the only documentation

One side note about tests: often TDD is stated as having the benefit of providing tests as part of the documentation, as they are the examples on how to use the code after all. This is often an excuse to not bother to write up any examples outside this and also to not document the overall design since reading the tests states the design.

The problem with this approach is that for the tests, all methods are equally important. It is very hard to convey an auxiliary decision made because it did not seem to have an impact at this moment from a core design idea of the project. This makes refactoring hard and is prone to side-track the project and maintain features that were never intended to be any in the beginning. For a developer coming into a project, the documentation should specify what the core functionality is, and if he or she finds a use for some obscure function outside this core, this is great and a good place for reading the tests, but there is a way to distinguish a feature that has support from the main application versus an auxiliary one.

One approach to try to make this more interactive is README-driven development, where we write the README first and make the examples executable, trying to make our code pass the examples we specified as the first layer of tests.

 You can read more on README-driven development at Tom Preston-Werner's blog, `http://tom.preston-werner.com/2010/08/23/readme-driven-development.html`.

Summary

In this chapter, we focused on the interaction between different subprojects forming sub-domains and collaborating with each other by different means. This collaboration can take many forms and depending on the context and the state of the application as a whole, some can be more valuable then others.

The right choice for collaboration is always up for debate, of course, and it is very possible to change the mode as the project evolves. An important point I would like to get across is that those collaboration ideas are not set in stone; it is a sliding scale and every team should decide what works best for them and what keeps the actual complexity in the application and the team work low.

In the last part, the chapter focused on the important things when creating documentation for a project and how we can make it useful while not diving into the realm of creating elaborate specifications that nobody ever touches or even understands as soon as they leave the hands of the architect who created them in the first place.

In the next chapter, we are going to explore how other development methods fit into domain-driven design, how a good object-oriented structure can support the design in general, and how domain-driven design is influenced by many other techniques.

7
It's Not All Domain-driven Design

If I have seen further, it is by standing on the shoulders of giants.

– Sir Isaac Newton

As with most things in developing, and not just when developing software, most concepts have been discovered before and most things have been done before, but there are those slight variations, or a recombination of ideas, that make old concepts more useful or enable new and innovative uses. The practice of developing software has been growing and evolving since the beginning. Some time ago, the concept of structured programming, the use of functions, subroutines, while and for loops, was considered a new concept. Later, object-orientation and functional programming took those ideas and added new ones on top to further ease maintainability and allow programmers to better express their intentions in the programs they write.

As with those ideas, domain-driven design evolved from a lot of the ideas of object-oriented programming, and a lot of them have been mentioned throughout the book already. There are more concepts influencing the ideas, and some of them are closely related to object-orientation, such as the ideas of aspect-orientation, and using plain objects to model a core service-layer in a system. But there are also ideas originating from other areas, such as building domain-specific languages. Domain-specific languages have been around for a very long time and they are commonly seen in the LISP family of languages.

The LISP family knows different forms of DSLs, and most LISP programs can be seen as a very lightweight DSL in themselves. Visit `http://en.wikipedia.org/wiki/Lisp_%28programming_language%29` for more details.

Functional programming also added to the ideas of domain-driven design, most notably the idea that immutability is a thing to aim for, easing debugging, and thinking about the domain in general.

In the following chapter, you will see in detail what those additional concepts are that influence domain-driven design, as well as programming in general. This chapter will cover the following topics:

- Understanding the prerequisites for domain-driven design
- Getting to know the influences such as object- and aspect-oriented programming, programming with plain objects, as well as command-query separation
- Domain-specific languages
- Other programming practices such as functional programming and event-based systems

Matching the domain to the problem

Working on an application mostly means thinking about ways to express a given problem in a way that a machine can understand and work on it. Domain-driven design takes this full circle back and makes sure that the people working on the domain understand the machine representation of the problem, and are therefore able to reason about it and contribute to it.

Throughout the book, we have been talking about building a language for humans and machines at the same time. Doing this means taking the constructs that JavaScript gives us and making them expressive to developers and domain experts alike.

There are many ways to express a problem, and some of them are easier to reason about than others. In a very simple case, for example, one could write the sum of the numbers of an array like this:

```
var ns = [1,2,3,4]
for(var i = ns.length-1, si = ns[i], s = 0; si = ns[i--];) s += si
console.log("sum for " + ns + " is " + s)
```

This simple program works by doing a lot of work inside the `for` loop check, assigning a current element of the array, an initial starting value for the sum, and consequently uses those to implement the sum. To make the loop a little more confusing, it uses the property of getting an index outside the array bounds, resulting in an undefined, which is false to break out of the loop in the check.

Even though this works, it is very hard to reason about what is happening. This is due to naming as well as complex constructs being used to express the idea of summing up numbers.

Growing into a domain

Thinking about the domain in the previous example, we can see that JavaScript already gives us terms to express this domain more clearly, assuming some familiarity with mathematical terms, for example:

```
var numbers = [1,2,3,4]
sum = numbers.reduce(function (a, b) { return a + b }, 0)
console.log("sum for " + numbers + " is " + sum)
```

By using the tools available to us, we can slowly grow into the domain concepts in general, extending what is already there, and building what needs to be added. We now use the built-in reduce function to do the same as the `for` loop did before. The `reduce` function takes a function as an argument, which gets passed the result so far and the current element, and we also give it a starting point of 0 to get the process started. For people familiar with the language, this is much more readable and almost instantly understandable as it uses the common concepts of how to express operations on arrays.

Using the same basic technique, we can leverage the built-in functions to accomplish tasks in our domain as well. When we want to calculate the time a transport takes, we might want to only consider the working days, so we need to filter weekends, and using the built-in function, this can be expressed cleanly:

```
var SATURDAY = 6
var SUNDAY = 7

var days = [1,2,3,4,5,6,7,8,9,10,11,12,13,14,15,16]

var transportTime = 11

var arrivalDay = days.filter(function (e) {
  if (e % SATURDAY === 0) return false
  if (e % SUNDAY === 0) return false
  return true
})[transportTime]
```

We use the filter method to filter out weekends in the days from now, assuming it is Monday, and we can then select the arrival day as the position in the array. As we move along in our development we can make this even clearer, but using the built-in methods to operate already gives the code natural readability.

Different domains have different merits of expressiveness, and the more understood a certain problem is, in general, the better it leads to building a domain design around the idea, in case when the general problem's complexity actually leads to a domain-driven design.

A good domain for domain-driven design

So far we have been working with the dungeon management system, which manages cells and prisoners coming in and out of the dungeon, making the dungeon money if they are present. This domain is quite complex as we have seen already, as we have just managed the transport of prisoners out of the dungeon so far, allowing the dungeon to have enough prisoners at the right time. This is, of course, not a real-world example, well obviously, as we have been talking about orcs. The example is grounded in a very real-world application, originally based on the idea of managing bookings for hotels, with over- and underbooking.

On inspecting the domain, we can see certain properties that make it a valuable domain for domain-driven design. The inherent problem is quite complex and involves many different parts to collaborate and model, to build a complete, working system. Each part is also commonly subject to change as the system is further optimized towards an optimal system, providing maximum profit for the using company.

What further increases the value of the domain design, in this case, is that the users interacting with the system vary widely. Different users need to be exposed to different interfaces being wired together. This kind of sharing functionality is hard to get right, and having a central core model to model the shared parts is a good way to keep the different sub-applications from drifting apart, which is a common problem in projects having a common set of domain-specific logic split over multiple applications.

The power of object-orientation

Large parts of the concepts we have been leveraging as part of our building of the application so far are by no means specific inventions for the concepts of domain-driven design. Many familiar with other work around these principles of software engineering will have noticed many ideas from other areas. A large chunk of ideas are those cultivated by many people over the years as part of object-orientation.

The object-oriented principles so far

Object-orientation is about the encapsulation of state with functionality. The idea is fundamental and we have been using it throughout the book to build up our system and compose different parts as objects. JavaScript objects are special when it comes to object-orientation, as JavaScript is one of the few languages based on prototypical inheritance versus classical inheritance like most other object-oriented languages. This means more than a special way to deal with inheritance; it also means that JavaScript has a very easy way to deal with objects. Because there is no real difference between an instance and a class, the syntax to deal with objects is very simple:

```
var thing = {
  state: 1,
  update: function() {
    this.state++
  }
}

thing.update()
thing.update()
thing.state          // => 3
```

This is the most simple way to create objects and is also the most often used one in JavaScript.

We have used objects to both represent value objects as well as entities, especially value objects. A key point to object-oriented programming is the isolation objects provide; when building the system we build it up by letting objects interact via sending messages to each other. This works particularly well when we are able to separate the command from the query messages as we have done. Splitting the commands from the queries enables easier testing and better reasoning about the code as it splits the things that modify the state (the commands) from idempotent operations (the queries that can be executed without causing any side effects). Another even more important advantage is that separating queries from commands allows us to express the significance of the commands from the domain more clearly. When we issue a command to a domain object, it has a significant meaning in the domain and should therefore stand on its own as well as being in the ubiquitous language established in the project. When issuing a command, we always want to express the "why", and bundling this with a query does not allow a name to express both.

A common example is the command to update a property on the object, like `updateAddress`, which does not tell us the "why" when naming it. `changeDeliveryTarget` makes it clearer why this attribute was updated. Mixing these kind of changes in a query method is unnatural.

Prototypical inheritance gives us another great way to model our data, as compared to classical inheritance the chains in prototypical inheritance are likely quite shallow. The important feature of prototypes is that they allow us to inherit dynamically from any object. The following code shows the usage of `Object.create` to inherit and extend objects:

```
var otherThing = Object.create(thing, {
  more: { value: "data" }
})

otherThing.update()
thing.update()

thing.state         // => 2
otherThing.state    // => 2
otherThing.more     // => data
thing.more          // => undefined
```

Using the `Object.create` method allows us to easily build from other objects. It was not always present in JavaScript, and before we needed to do a lot more to get the same effect, but with the `Object.create` method, building objects is very natural and it embraces the concept of prototypical inheritance.

Objects lend themselves very well to model data that flows through the system as they are very lightweight and extendable. There are a couple of caveats we need to be aware of, as discussed in the previous sections. Especially, the simple extension that allows the use of shallow inheritance hierarchies while still using polymorphism to resolve control flow. Using polymorphism to control the control flow is the common approach in object-orientation to allow objects to encapsulate knowledge. When we send a command to an object, we want it to act according to its internal knowledge and state, and we don't care about its specific implementation unless we want to send it a specific command. This allows us to have smart objects that respond to commands directed at them differently, for example:

```
var counter = {
  state: 1,
  update: function() {
    this.state++
  }
}

var jumpingCounter = Object.create(counter, {
  update: { value: function() { this.state += 10 } }
})

jumpingCounter.update()
jumpingCounter.state // => 11
```

We again use a basic JavaScript object as the base to build new functionality on top. This time, we extend our simple counter with new functionality by implementing a jumping counter with a new function, without modifying the underlying counter object. This shows the power of easy extensibility—we can just use functionality encapsulated in objects that already exist and build upon it without much ceremony. This possibility is the source of much of the power of JavaScript, a nice power to have but also easily abused.

This leads to a very simple model of domain models that depend on each other, which can be used directly but also extended along the way.

The object-oriented modeling of business domains

The idea of object-orientation to encapsulate the business domain is of great benefit in general as it leads to a less coupled system that is easier to understand and modify. When we think of objects as things we pass messages to and receive answers from, we naturally couple ourselves less to the internal structure of the code, as the API becomes a question and answer, as well as a command game.

In a very simple example going back to our dungeon and its orcs, we might want to implement a method for fighting an intruder. So we start by implementing an orc with a weapon, using a very lightweight object to start with, for example:

```
var Orc = {
  init: function (name, weapon) {
    this.name = name
    this.weapon = weapon
    return this
  },

  get isArmed () { return !!this.weapon },

  attack: function (opponent) {
    console.log(this.name + " strikes "
        + opponent.name + " with " + this.weapon + ".")
  }
}
```

There is one feature here that is not commonly used but is very powerful: we can define getters and setters in JavaScript for objects via the special get or set syntax, allowing us to first of all limit the scope of modifications to our properties, but also to allow us to construct more complex properties out of other ones. In this case, we abstract the knowledge that a missing weapon means the orc is not armed.

We consider the fight to be its own domain object, so we model it as well:

```
var Fight = {
  init: function (orc, attacker) {
    this.orc = orc
    this.attacker = attacker
    return this
  },

  round: function () {
    if (this.orc.isArmed) {
      this.orc.attack(this.attacker)
    } else {
      this.attacker.attack(this.orc)
    }
  }
}
```

The fight encapsulates the logic that only an armed orc can actually attack his opponent during a battle. This is, of course, very simple logic but it might grow to be more complex. We will use an object model to abstract away the fact of how a fight is handled in the system.

 It is always important to keep in mind that creating objects, especially in JavaScript, is very cheap. Encapsulating too much knowledge into one object is not a good idea and more often than not, it is better to split an object early into responsibilities. A good indicator for this is an object that has lots of private methods, or methods whose names are closely related.

We can now model our fight with the objects:

```
var agronak = Object.create(Orc).init("Agronak", "sword")
var traugh = Object.create(Orc).init("Traugh")

var fight = Object.create(Fight).init(agronak, traugh)
fight.round() // => Agronak strikes Traugh with sword.
```

This encapsulates the logic for the fight in its own object and uses the orcs to encapsulate logic related to the orcs.

The scenarios of pure object-orientation falling short

The basics of object orientation work very well for large parts of modeling the domain. Especially in JavaScript with its very lightweight object creation and modeling, it lends itself quite nicely to model a domain like we have seen.

Where object orientation falls short is on the level of transaction management, we have certain interaction spanning multiple objects that needs to be managed from a higher level. On the other hand, we don't want the details of the transaction to leak to all the involved objects. This is where domain-driven design comes in with a separation of value objects, entities, and aggregates. In this case, aggregates allow workflow management by being the life-cycled manager of other collaborators. As we model the domain as composed of sub-domains, even though an entity may be shared between different collaborating sub-domains, each sub-domain has its own view of the entity. In each sub-domain, an aggregate can control the transactions necessary to accomplish the task and make sure the data is in a consistent state.

There are, of course, multiple other additions as we have seen throughout the book but the addition of a higher-level management for the lower-level details of the objects is an important feature, extending object-oriented application structures toward domain-driven form object orientation.

Influences to keep close

Object-orientation is not the only influence on application development we have seen throughout the book. Many different techniques can be useful to model domain concepts and influence how applications are developed. JavaScript itself is a very flexible language and can be used, and sometimes to abused, to do very interesting things.

Depending on the situation, different ideas can be good to keep at hand when modeling certain aspects or solving certain problems as they occur when building the model.

Aspect-oriented programming

At its core, most ideas of software development revolve around how it is possible to encapsulate logic and state it so it is easily accessible and has a common interface that is understandable as well as extensible. Extensibility is a very important aspect especially in business software since the requirements need to be adjusted to the real world and the software needs to be able to encompass new requirements quickly.

Aspect-oriented programming sets the idea of aspects of the software development in the centre of the program design, and concerns itself especially with how we can implement cross-cutting concerns without duplication and in a maintainable fashion. Aspects in the case of aspect-oriented programming are all kind of concerns that might be shared across different objects.

The canonical example of aspect-oriented programming is the addition of an audit log to the system. The audit log is something that would need to be implemented across all the different domain objects, while at the same time not being a core concern to the object. Aspect-oriented programming extracts the aspect, in this case the audit logging, and applies it to each object that should be treated this way. By that means, it makes the aspect a core part of the system, decoupled from the business object.

JavaScript, due to its very dynamic nature, can do this very simply and dynamically; one solution is to use traits.

 The traits used are based on `https://javascriptweblog.wordpress.com/2011/05/31/a-fresh-look-at-javascript-mixins/`.

We can now build on the previous example and add `audit` logging to our `Fight` object. We can add the calls to the log to the `fight` class directly:

```
var util = require("util")

var Fight = {
  init: function (orc, attacker, audit) {
    this.audit = audit
    if (this.audit) {
      console.log("Called init on " + util.inspect(this) + " with
" + util.inspect(arguments))
    }
    this.orc = orc
    this.attacker = attacker
    return this
  },
```

```
round: function () {
  if (this.audit) {
    console.log("Called round on " + util.inspect(this) + " with
" + util.inspect(arguments))
  }
    if(this.orc.isArmed) {
      this.orc.attack(this.attacker)
    } else {
      this.attacker.attack(this.orc)
    }
  }
}
```

To make sure we can either audit the fight or not, we will add a flag and then check and log the appropriate calls. This adds quite a lot of plumbing to the object as we also now need to depend on a way to inspect, and therefore add a dependency, to the util library.

I consider flag arguments a red flag in most cases as they indicate that multiple concerns are mixed in one place, which need to be switched on. Often, it can be an indicator of a cross-cutting concern better solved by using aspect-orientation.

A better way to add logging to the orc fight is by adding a loggable trait to the fight. The trait would be the following:

```
var util = require("util")

var asLoggable = function () {
  Object.keys(this).forEach(function (key) {
    if (this.hasOwnProperty(key) && typeof this[key] ===
' function' ) {
      var that = this
      var fn = this[key]
      this[key] = function () {
        console.log("Called " + key + " on " + util.inspect(that)
+ " with " + util.inspect(arguments))
        return fn.apply(that, arguments)
      }
    }
  }, this)
  return this
}
```

The code wraps each function in a function that first logs its arguments and forwards them to the function afterwards. This is possible without touching the object at all in an abstract way since JavaScript allows us to enumerate all the properties of the object we want to extend via the introspection capabilities.

When applied to an object, the `asLoggable` trait wraps every method of the object in a logged method, writing out which function was called on what, and with what kind of arguments, and to output more meaningful information, it uses the `inspect` library.

Let's apply this to the previously constructed code, which means replacing the `Fight` object with the `LoggableFight` object:

```
var LoggableFight = asLoggable.call(Fight)
var fight = Object.create(LoggableFight).init(agronak, traugh)
fight.round()
```

The calls will now be logged and the output will be as follows, but shortened for printability:

```
Called init on { init:…, round:…} with { … }
Called round on {…, orc: {…}, attacker: {…} } with {}
Agronak strikes Traugh with sword.
```

This addition does not change the overall behavior, but is a pure extension to the system.

Extending an object in this way is a very powerful technique but can be quite dangerous at the same time. Even though the code is quite simple to create, it is not as easy to understand where certain properties of the code come from, and a lot depends on the right naming. If we, for example, had just replaced the `Fight` object all together, getting rid of the `LoggableFight` object name, there would be no indication of why there is suddenly logging applied to the method, and a developer tracking down a bug in the code would have a tough time in a big project.

Command-query separation

While aspect-orientation is about separating concerns at the level of objects, command query separation is about separating concerns at the level of methods. We have seen before that handling the state is difficult and a value object is therefore more simple than an entity. The same is true for methods: sending a query to an object means that the object will answer the same query in the same way as long as it holds the same state, and the query does not modify the state. This makes it very easy to write tests for queries because a simple setup of the object, and asserting the output of the method, does the trick.

Commands can be more complicated, as they modify the state of the object that they are sent to. A command in general does not have a return value but should only result in a state change for the object. This again makes it easier for us to test the result of commands, as we can set up an object, send a command, and assert that the appropriate change has been applied, without having to assert at the same time that the correct return value has been returned along the way. What we need to keep in mind when writing commands is to manage their failure states, and depending on the application there are multiple ways to deal with this. The simplest way might be raising an exception, or when using `async` commands, returning an error to the callback. This allows managing the aggregate, to react and either roll back, or handle the problem appropriately. Either way, we don't want to return more complex results as this quickly leads down the path of depending on data being returned from the command.

Command-query separation is one of the core principles to keep in mind when writing maintainable code that can be tested and extended.

Plain old objects

Along with the separation comes the tendency to make things as simple as possible, and the way to go for most applications, especially in JavaScript, is to use the simple, plain objects that JavaScript provides. We have multiple ways to construct objects in JavaScript, and throughout the book we have been using both the classical and more more class-like pattern:

```
function Orc(name) {
  this.name = name
}

Orc.prototype.introduce = function () {
  console.log("I AM " + this.name + "!")
}
```

In this chapter, we also used the more JavaScript-like pattern using `Object.create` and exemplar objects.

The important thing to note in all of this is that the code stays away from using complex containers to manage the objects, the lifecycle, and more. Using plain objects, whatever pattern is used to construct them, means they can be tested in isolation and are simple to follow through the application, as well as extensively using the patterns of the core language as needed.

Domain-specific languages

Using specific keywords to describe parts of the domain is one of the main goals we set out to achieve in building a system using domain-driven design. Especially the LISP community, which has been an influence on JavaScript (http://readwrite. com/2011/07/22/javascript-was-no-accident), there is a strong tendency to meld the language to the problem. This naturally leads to further trying to make the language fit the domain, with the ultimate goal of having a language that is perfect for solving the specific problem the domain has.

This kind of development is referred to as using **Domain-specific Languages**, or **DSL** for short. In day-to-day work, there are lots of very DSLs we come across, be it CSS to describe the style of a HTML document, or SQL for interfacing with the database. The lines when a language is a DSL and when it is a general-purpose language are often a bit blurred. SQL, for example, is often considered a "real" programming language, so to speak, even though it has the very specific purpose of modifying and querying a relational database.

A DSL is often defined and implemented on a host language and a library to provide the functionality first, and is then further refined by adding a special syntax on top. A more recent example of this can be seen in the Ruby world where the server administration toolkit Chef started out as a library of functions to control the configuration of servers, but as this developed the system became more DSL-like and by now, the language to describe configuration is still hosted on Ruby but has its own words to describe the specifics of server administration. The power of this model is, of course, that the underlying language is still Ruby, a general-purpose language, and therefore when the DSL reaches its limits, there is always the possibility to extend it using the host language.

Creating DSLs

This kind of model is what we would want to follow in a system in my opinion. When building a new application, it is not practical to start designing a DSL to solve the—at this point probably still unknown—core problem of the domain. But we want to start building a library of words we can use to describe our problem, gluing this kind of library together more and more, while filling in the gaps. This is how most (good) DSLs evolve. They start as a library and grow until they reach a point where it becomes practical to extract the language itself as a core domain part.

JavaScript itself is full of DSLs, as the language design lends itself very nicely to the construction of libraries that expose their functionality as a DSL. The line, again, is not always clear but as we look at code such as the following, we can see a certain DSL-like nature. The following snippet is an example from `https://jquery.com/`:

```
var $hiddenBox = $( "#banner-message" );
$( "#button-container button" ).on( "click", function( event ) {
  $hiddenBox.show();
});
```

The code uses the **jQuery** selection engines to define click handlers on elements, and trigger actions in them.

jQuery has become one of those almost ubiquitous libraries and is almost considered essential by some web developers. jQuery first introduced the way to select certain page elements by their selector, be it "#" for an element ID or "." for elements by class. This way of reusing the selector definition from CSS to also select elements from the page, and therefore being able with one function—the $, to create a language to manipulate all kinds of page elements, is the real power of jQuery.

DSLs in domain-driven design

As we are looking at other DSLs, we should realize that our own approach for development hasn't been too far from the power of a true DSL. There is some way to go of course, but even the simple examples from the beginning of the chapter show where we are going in accordance to naming things right, to be able to grow a language we can speak with the domain experts. This is another power of DSLs as the goal is to make the language as understandable as possible to people not considered the core developers of the system.

Where jQuery made it possible for web designers to start manipulating their web pages with JavaScript, our language in the project should make it possible for the business owners to check whether the rules that are supposed to be reflected by the system are truly reflected as they are supposed to be. The following code shows how we can use our build functions, to clearly show in the code how a prisoner transfer is executed:

```
prisonerTransfer = function (prisoner, otherDungeon, ourDungeon,
notifier, callback) {
  var keeper = ourDungeon.getOrc()
  var carriage = ourDungeon.getCarriage()
  var transfer = prepareTransfer(carriage, keeper, prisoner)
  if (transfer) {
    notifier.message(otherDungeon, transfer)
    callback()
```

```
  } else {
    callback(new Error("Transfer initiation failed."))
  }
}
```

Even though a business expert would likely not understand the preceding code directly, it allows us to follow through with an explanation. We can explain the inputs to the expert saying, "A prisoner transfer involves the prisoner being sent, the dungeon the prisoner is sent to and the dungeon the prisoner is coming from. We also need notify the dungeon". Walking through the code, we can explain the steps along the way:

1. A prisoner is supposed to be transferred from one dungeon to another.

2. We need a keeper and a carriage to perform the transfer.

3. If the transfer succeeds, a message is sent to the dungeon.

These simple-to-follow rules, stated as closely as possible to plain English, is what we are aiming for. Even though we might not involve the business experts in daily code walkthroughs, it is useful to be able to cross-check the rules as close to the code when the need arises, and just to reduce our own mental overhead.

Drawing knowledge

Object orientation and its specific forms are, of course, not the only influence we have, and not the only one we should have. Many different ways of developing software have been found to be useful and have value in the world of software development. Depending on the kind of system we want to build, it is not always the best even to model as objects.

There are very common ways that lend themselves nicely to specific problems, be it a more functional approach when faced with the problems of concurrency, or a more logical approach when trying to build a rule engine. All these kind of ways to approach a problem influence the way we think about a system, and the more different approaches there are in our toolbox, the better we can pick one that fits.

Naturally, certain approaches feel better for an individual; I, for example, don't fair well when faced with a purely functional, statically-typed approach that, for example, Haskell takes to developing software. I have a hard time expressing my thoughts about the problem in such a language. Don't get discouraged by this kind of struggle though, because even your day-to-day work might not seem to fit the approach, you might come across a problem where it fits perfectly.

For this reason, I think that besides knowing about the approaches that object orientation takes to solve problems, close relation to domain-driven design, can't be the end all, and an introduction to other ways of thinking can be very helpful to draw knowledge from.

Functional programming

> *Functional programming is a style of programming which models computations as the evaluation of expressions.*
>
> *-https://wiki.haskell.org/Functional_programming*

Functional programming has gained a lot of influence over the last years, and it has not only gained traction in niche communities, but companies have been founded on the idea that functional programming is a way to develop software.

Even though it has been around for a long time, a recent surge of interest in the ideas of functional programming has been sparked, but problems arise in the development of large scale systems needing to serve large numbers of users concurrently, and be as bug free as possible. The premise of functional programming is that large parts of the development can be done in a purely functional way, avoiding mutation of the state as well as passing around functions to be executed on other functions, or value objects to be transformed toward the end result.

As our systems become more parallel and have to deal with more concurrent requests, the more functional our code is and the more it interacts with immutable data structures, the easier to manage this increasingly complex scenario gets. We can avoid the need for more complex locking, as well as race conditions that are hard to debug.

Functional programming and JavaScript

JavaScript has had many influences, be it the prototypical inheritance mechanism oriented towards the way inheritance is done in the language itself, or the way functions are first class citizens as they are in **Scheme**, a LISP dialect.

This influence from Scheme makes JavaScript somewhat functional even though it is, maybe, not the primary focus of the way many people use the language:

```
var numbers = [1,2,3,4,5,6]

var result = numbers.map(function(number) {
  return (number * 2)
}).filter(function(e) {
```

```
    return (e % 2) === 0
}).reduce(function(acc, val) {
    return acc + val
})

result // => a number, like 40
```

In the beginning of this chapter, we already used the `reduce` function on the array, and we can now follow this up with a `filter` and `map` to create more complex chains of operations. These all work very similarly and abstract away the knowledge of how iteration should be handled, but they let you express the action to be done. In the case of a map, transforming each element to its square, and in the case of a filter, sorting out elements that do not match a certain criteria.

JavaScript has basic ways to operate on elements in a functional style. Using the likes of map, reduce, and filter, we can quickly modify collections, for example, and this kind of programming is often used to modify sets of HTML elements in a similar style.

Of course, a program like this could also be written as a `for` loop, but in this case the intention gets lost in the setup of the loop as well as the management of the loop variables. Functional methods specialized in modifying collections are a very effective way to boil the problem down to the core steps and describe them as functions to apply, without having to worry about how each element is mapped over, selected from the original collection and, probably most importantly, where to store the result.

For increased readability, we can name the functions being applied, as required, to reduce the mental overhead for the reader having to understand the function body. Combined with the higher abstraction level, these collection methods, like the previously introduced methods such as `filter` and `reduce`, mean we can quickly create very expressive APIs.

Value objects

The idea that we don't want to worry about where we store results but simply operate on the input and let the language figure out what to do about the intermediate results, and how to manage the pass through of the elements, is a core strength of functional programming. Even though this is not the case for JavaScript, it is easy to see how the preceding code could be optimized by the compiler to pass through items in batches, or even operate on the items in separate workers instead of letting the main process do all the work.

These kinds of optimizations are easy to do when we don't have to directly deal with the problems of concurrency. The main problem of concurrency is the shared state between different parts of the program. So the main thing to learn from functional approaches is possibly the idea that what we called "value objects" before, objects that are only identified by their properties and not their identity, are a good thing. We can easily pass them around and modify collections of them with functions, and share them with whoever we want, because they can't change.

Value objects make dependencies shallow, as they terminate chains we have to think about. Once we reach a value object, we can be sure that we just need to construct one in case we want to test something. There is no need for mocking, stubbing, or anything complicated.

Not only are value objects at the core of functional approaches, maybe as much as the idea that functions are a first class thing, but they are also there to represent the data to pass through the system. As we have seen before, this data can flow through, instead of having to stop and be evaluated as a whole. This thinking naturally leads to another tool in our tool chest, using events to model the state of a system.

Events

The real-world functions through a system of reactions to actions and events. If somebody wants me to open the door of my apartment, they will ring the doorbell, and if I'm at home, I will react to this and go to open the door. This is a well-defined flow of events: first somebody decides they want to trigger me to open the door, so they need to discover the service to send the event, in this case the doorbell, they then trigger the event by pressing the doorbell. When I hear the ring, I first need to check whether the event is actually for me, and in the case of the doorbell this depends on whether I'm alone at home or not. After deciding that the event is actually for me, I can decide how to react, selecting the appropriate handler, so to speak, so I will get up and go to open the door.

At each point of the execution, I can decide how to handle the next step. If I am in the shower, for example, I might decide to ignore the event and just continue showering. After I'm done, I might check the door later, queuing up the action to handle the event. Also in the case of the doorbell, the event is multicast to multiple consumers; if, for example, my wife is at home, she can also go to open the door. From an event-sender side, we also have multiple options: if I'm outside somebody's house, I can decide to ring the doorbell, but if I don't get a reaction, I can check whether there are other ways to trigger the signal; I can, for example, just knock. The following diagram shows the flow of events described:

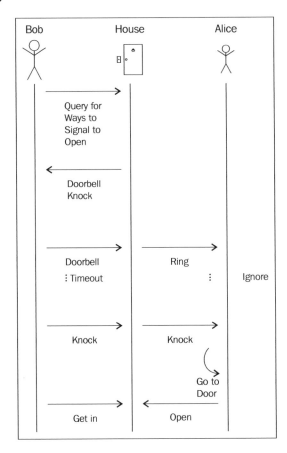

This little example shows the very power of modeling a system via small components communicating via events. Each component can decide how to respond to an event considering its current load or even other events being triggered at the same time. Priorities can be implemented by reordering the events either on the sender side or on the consumer side to ensure the best responsiveness for the system in regards to the agreed-upon service level agreements.

JavaScript offers this kind of eventing at its core, and NodeJS's EventEmitter is a nice abstraction over the core idea, leading to very clear code, for example:

```
var EventEmitter = require("events").EventEmitter
var util = require("util")

function House() {
  EventEmitter.call(this)

  var that = this

  this.pleaseOpen = function() {
    // use the EventEmitter to send the ring event
    that.emit("ring")
  }
}

util.inherits(House, EventEmitter)

var me = {
  onRing: function(ev) {
        console.log("opening door")
      }
}

var myHouse = new House()
// subscribe to the ring event, and dispatch it
myHouse.on("ring", me.onRing)

myHouse.pleaseOpen()
```

The EventEmitter function allows us to add to the functionality commonly known from interacting with the document object model in JavaScript to any object we need. In the preceding code, we use the inherits helper to make our House be an EventEmitter. With this in place, we can act on events and dispatch them as seen. We can define events we want other objects to be able to react to, like we would react to clicks or hover events.

Event stores versus entity relational mapping

Depending on what our system is supposed to achieve, it can be important to save events. In the case of our doorbell example where I am in the shower, we might have the problem that I can not hear the event as well as my decision to not respond to it. Depending on the reason the person triggering the event had, this can either be acceptable or not.

If it were the postman trying to drop off a package and they don't want to wait, they can have a short timeout to await a response and if they don't get one, they can queue the package delivery again on their side, get back in the van, and try again tomorrow. In other circumstances when we want the system delivering the event to handle this scenario for us, this is also common, for example, when I miss a call, I will get an SMS with the call details, or a voicemail saving the event details for me and when I'm ready to handle it I can do so.

In many software systems, we want the event delivery system to abstract away as many things as possible. Going all the way to the extreme, it is even possible to construct the system purely by storing the events and never actually modifying any data, but just generating new events to again be stored. All the system needs to know at this point is at which point in time a consumer is in regards to the event stream, and it can then replay whatever is needed, obviating the need to store modifiable data by mapping entities to a database. The only entity in this scenario is the pointer into the event log for each consumer. This is not something that is easy to implement as it raises problems due to the only eventually consistent nature of such a system. After all, it takes time to send events between systems, but it might be worth it for a reasonably complex system to tackle.

 A very good example of such a system is **Kafka**, and it is a whole ecosystem for modeling, consuming, event creation, and storage, but there are other examples for this as well. Martin Kleppman has written about, and presented on this, at various occasions, for example, at Spanconf 2014: https://www.youtube.com/watch?v=b_H4FFE3wP0.

Creating a system like this is probably not the simplest or the first choice when developing a business application as the requirements for the infrastructure to support it are quite high. The more the application has to deal with high availability and the more the system starts to be distributed for whatever reason, the more reasonable such a system becomes. JavaScript as a language is very well suited to event handling, as it is at the core of the domain the language was build for—reacting to user events in the browser.

Further reading

Throughout this chapter, there have been a lot of things introduced that are not the primary focus but still added a great deal of understanding to the evolvement of domain-driven design. Being inspired by workarounds can really improve the general software development practices so there is further reading I would recommend. To further understand object orientation, and especially to find design patterns to use, I recommend the book called *Gang of four*, and *Design Patterns : Elements of Reusable Object-Oriented Software, Erich Gamma, Richard Helm, Ralph Johnson, John Vlissides, Pearson Publishing*. Even though the book is old, it still represents classic work on object orientation, and establishes a lot of terminology. Also *Smalltalk Best Practice Patterns, Kent Becks, Prentice Hall*, really embraces Object-Oriented design, and even though both books are naturally not focused on JavaScript, they can still be very helpful in advancing your design skills.

At the other end of the chapter, we went into some detail on how to get started on modeling a flow of events, which is currently a very hot topic. Martin Kleppmann has been doing a lot of work around this area, so following his work closely will bring you some good insights into how to model growing applications (`https://martin.kleppmann.com/`).

There is obviously a lot more to follow up on, but getting started with the mentioned work will naturally lead to a lot more, probably more than is digestible in a short amount of time, so I recommend you go and follow this up and follow it down the rabbit hole.

Summary

In this chapter, we looked at the various ways domain-driven design is influenced and can be augmented by related software development patterns. Some patterns are closer than others, such as DSLs, and some are more orthogonal such as modeling the system as a series of events.

The important thing is to make sure we don't get stuck in trying to only apply the techniques we see in a specific pattern, but look at what is around to make sure we use the right tool for the job. At its core, domain-driven design is about modeling business software, and while most business software follows similar patterns and rules, some internal details might be very well-suited for a functional core integrated in the software as a whole, or even the development of a DSL that allows not-so-technical business experts to express their rules clearly.

In the next chapter, we are going to sum up all the details we came across and are going to think about how to work on an ever-changing product like most business software is.

8

Seeing It All Come Together

All software projects are special and there can never be a "one size fits all" approach, but as we have seen, a lot of thought has gone into all kinds of different approaches to development. A project goes through many stages of development, often it starts out exploring the basic ideas, sometimes we can not even be sure at that stage what the domain of the project will be. We then begin to factor out a certain core competency of the application and a core domain starts to evolve. At this stage the involvement of the business experts is crucial to make sure the domain aligns with the business needs, and the project does not get sidetracked due to misunderstandings, while the ubiquitous language is evolving along the way. The project tends to grow from one or two developers to a larger team, and team organization becomes more important since we need to start thinking about the communication overhead involved in the development as the assumption that everybody is familiar with more or less everything in the codebase no longer holds true. At this point a team can decide to go for a domain-driven approach and start to really model the now established domain in more detail. Even though the involvement of the business experts might not be needed every day in the later stages, a consistent involvement is important to make sure a project does not depart from the core domain needs.

This idealized form of project growth is dependent on multiple environmental factors, not only does the team have to be set up to make the choices described, the application also needs to be ready for the approach. We've seen previously that not all projects work well with a domain-driven approach, and there are many different kinds of JavaScript projects, which can fit the approach at different stages of development.

In this chapter we are taking a look at the different projects, some domains, and how those two things, together with domain-driven design, fit the whole picture. We will be exploring:

- The different kind of project, that involve JavaScript
- How client- and server-side development influences projects
- The different problems and their suitability for domain-driven design
- Example domains for domain-driven design

The different kinds of JavaScript project

JavaScript, as a very versatile language, made its way through the different stages of development. Originally conceived as a way to enable more dynamic behavior in the browser, it has conquered not only the complex field of developing, almost thick with client-like applications using the browser as the platform and runtime, but it is now also seen in server-side applications most prominently using Node.js.

Going all the way from making a document look more interactive by incorporating effects, to rendering a whole application on the client side is a wide spectrum of complexity and applications. Some may warrant an approach with a larger focus on application-design, some might best be served by smaller script-like approaches keeping the logic simple and local for the best maintenance.

Enhancing the user experience

Many business applications are perfectly well served by an application comprised of a number of pages all rendered on the server side. For the longest times this has been the way to go, and still is most likely the simplest approach as it keeps the stack of technologies to a minimum. As soon as the pages start to get complex it can help the user experience a lot to add some dynamic elements. Those elements can be for pointing out features or to guide the user. It can be very useful to do some client-side validation of the input for example, so the user does not send an obvious invalid request and has to wait for a slow response from the server:

```
<form>
  <label>
    Check Me: <input type="checkbox" id="check-me"></input>
  </label>
  <button id="disable-me">
    I can be clicked if you checked the box
  </button>
</form>
```

A form like this can be seen often, we want to prevent the user from being able to click the button until a checkbox is checked, and also maybe something needs to be agreed on before the request is valid. Having the validation on the server side is important, but giving some feedback to the user before hitting the button will be a great enhancement. A small JavaScript function, such as the following, can easily accomplish that:

```javascript
window.onload = function () {
  var checkMeBox = document.getElementById("check-me")
  var disableMeBtn = document.getElementById("disable-me")

  function checkBoxHandler() {
    if(checkMeBox.checked) {
        disableMeBtn.removeAttribute("disabled")
      } else {
        disableMeBtn.setAttribute("disabled", "true")
      }
    }

  checkBoxHandler()
  checkMeBox.onclick = checkBoxHandler
}
```

We check the value of the checkbox and deactivate or activate the button as needed.

This is a business rule and we want to see it reflected in the code; on the other hand, the rule is also enforced on the server side, so the need to make it work beyond any doubt does not arise. Problems like these arise often in applications, and we don't want to reach for overpowered tools straight away. If we, for example, start designing the form object as a business object, and encapsulating the rule for whether the form is *send-able* or not, we would arrive at an arguably cleaner design, at the readability cost of the code. This is the constant trade-off present at projects that are largely UX enhancements. In general, mixing view-code with business rules is not good; on the other hand, over-engineering very small enhancements, such as the preceding code, gets easily lost in the overhead of creating a more complex infrastructure for a cleaner model.

UX enhancements like this one don't lend themselves nicely to a domain-driven approach, since the knowledge about the business logic will have to be replicated, with a separate adapter for the HTML representation and the server-model representation. Adapters like this create some overhead and, depending on the amount of functionality encapsulated, they do not necessarily make sense. As the code on the client side grows and moves more toward an application, it starts to make more sense.

Single-page applications

In recent years, the concept of a thick client application has become more common again. In the early days of the Web, websites were static and later were enhanced using JavaScript to ease navigation or basic user interactions. In recent years, client-side applications in the browser started to grow to a level where a lot of business logic lived on the frontend, and the frontend itself became a true application.

 A long time ago, when the world still revolved around Mainframes, clients in a computing environment were often dumb terminals accepting the user input and showing the output. As the hardware grew more powerful, more and more business logic was moved to the client for processing, until we reached true client-side applications such as running Microsoft Office. We can see the same again in the browser now, as applications have become more complex and the browsers more capable.

A one-page application often implements large pieces of the business logic all implemented in JavaScript to serve as the thick client querying the server. Examples for such applications are plenty, ranging from the more traditional document-oriented style all the way to in-browser applications using HTML, CSS, and JavaScript as their runtime environment, taking over the browser more or less completely.

When developing an in-browser application, the structure of the underlying code matters a lot more than when enhancing some functionality of a webpage. The problem space is divided into several pieces. First, the code needs to be organized in such a way that it stays maintainable over a longer period of time as the applications grow and change. As the frontend application code now realizes bigger parts of the business logic, the maintenance burden grows and the risk of rewriting bigger parts grows with it. The application presents a major investment in the system. Second, even though the technology stack in the client seems fairly fixed with HTML, CSS, and JavaScript, best practices and browser support for features are evolving at a rapid pace. At the same time, backwards compatibility is crucial as developers don't have much control over the upgrade process of the users. Third, the performance aspect of a client-side application is important. Even though there have been massive strides in the speedup of JavaScript runtime engines, the users are expecting more and more from the applications and, more importantly, are running more and more applications in parallel as well. We can't expect our one-page application to own large parts of the machine it is running on, but we must be careful about spending resources.

The contrast of increased need for performance versus the need for flexibility is a driving factor in the development of frameworks and techniques to support the development of client-side applications. We want a framework to be flexible while at the same time refraining from over-abstraction, which may be costly in terms of performance for our applications. On the other hand, our users expect an increased amount of interactivity that requires more and more complex application code to manage as the client-side applications grow.

Different frameworks and their implications

The world of JavaScript frameworks is very vast, new frameworks with different promises are released constantly and abandoned constantly as well. All frameworks have their use cases and, while advocating different architectures, all consider providing a way to organize your JavaScript application essential.

On one side, there are small frameworks, or micro-frameworks, that are almost library-like, providing just a bare minimum of organization and abstraction. The most well known and probably most widely used of these is Backbone. The goal is to provide a way to route a user on the client side—handling the URL, and rewriting and updating the application state in the browser. On the other hand, the state is encapsulated into models, providing and abstracting the data access to the internal client-side state, as well as the remote server-side state, so a sync of these two can be managed.

On the other end of the spectrum, we find larger application frameworks, a popular one being Ember, providing a more integrated development experience in the browser. Handling data sync, routing too many different controllers in application pages, as well as an advanced view layer rendering different objects to the browser via templates including data binding between the interface and the backend model representation. This is very much along the lines of the old school approach of Smalltalk, such as the Model View Controller pattern.

A simple application using Ember for giving names to our orcs could work like this:

```
window.App = Ember.Application.create()

App.Orc = Ember.Object.extend({
  name: "Garrazk"
})

App.Router.map(function () {
  this.route(' index' , { path: ' /' })
})
```

```
var orc

App.IndexRoute = Ember.Route.extend({
  templateName: 'orc',
  controllerName: 'orc',
  model: function() {
    if(!orc) orc = App.Orc.create();
    return orc
  }
});

var names = [ "Yahg", "Hibub", "Crothu", "Rakgu", "Tarod",
"Xoknath", "Gorgu", "Olmthu", "Olur", "Mug" ]

App.OrcController = Ember.Controller.extend({
  actions: {
    rename: function () {
      var newName = names[Math.floor(Math.random()*names.length)];
      this.set("model.name", newName)
    }
  }
})
```

A top-level application manages the context, and we then define routes and controllers like we do in most MVC applications. This model scales quite well and allows for very different applications. The advantage is that we can rely a lot on prebuilt infrastructure. For example, in the preceding code, the wiring between the route and the controller can be setup quite easily, with the declarative assigning templateName and controllerName to use. Also, the wiring with the view is almost done, allowing us to define the main application template as follows:

```
<html>
  <head>
    <script src="http://code.jquery.com/jquery-
1.11.3.min.js"></script>
    <script src="http://builds.emberjs.com/release/ember-template-
compiler.js"></script>
    <script src="http://builds.emberjs.com/release/ember.min.js"></
script>
    <script src="/app.js"></script>
  </head>
  <script type="text/x-handlebars" data-template-name="orc">
    <p> ORC! {{ name }} </p>
    <button {{action "rename"}}>Give me a Name!</button>
  </script>
</html>
```

Using `Handlebars.js` for templating, and using the `preassign` model for interaction, Ember is designed to scale quite large frontend applications, taking over the browser interactions and providing a complete application framework.

Along the lines of this, we can find almost everything in between. In a world of domain-driven development, we now have to choose what best suits our application and our style of development. It may seem like a smaller framework is better suited to domain-driven design, as it allows the developer to have more influence, this is not necessarily the case. The important thing for us should be the way we can hook into the framework. The same way we interact with it server-side, we want to abstract our code as simple JavaScript objects, seeing the framework as a layer for us to get the content for the user displayed and the input from the user back in our domain layer. We want our domain layer to be separated from the framework as best as possible. With the growing prevalence of model-view-controller and alike organizations in today's developments, the frameworks allow for a better separation organization-wise as long as we don't fall into the trap of developing around the framework, but stick with the discussed organization as plain objects outside the framework hooking in to the framework as an implementation of a needed functionality.

Rendering on the client side

Depending on the application we are developing, going for a full client-side application might not be the way to go. Most business applications are, in the end, very task oriented, manipulating data via forms and triggering some logic based on this input. The result of the operations is then reflected in a document-like fashion. This represents how most business is done, it involves a process to accomplish a task, and ends with a report. Thinking about the application we have been working on throughout the book, we see a similar pattern. The part of the application we have been working on the most consists of several steps involving the dungeon master triggering a certain action by filling in details about a transport that is supposed to take place. The backend then decides if the conditions are met and if the request can be fulfilled and triggers the appropriate action. Most of the logic lives on the server side of the application, and due to consistency concerns, needs to live there as well. On the other hand, the client side is very form-oriented, the tasks involve one or more form steps that need to be accomplished according to the process for a given task. The logic for the process and the task is on the server, so a full client-side application will need to duplicate a lot of the server knowledge to give a client-side application feeling, but then we will still need to check with the backend for confirmation. This obviates the benefit of moving logic to the client side to a large degree.

In situations like this, a middle ground approach can make a lot of sense, ensuring that the advanced debugging capabilities and monitoring of the server side can be leveraged while still giving a more fluid feeling to the application. The idea is to render the snippets of HTML to be placed on the page, but place them on the page via JavaScript, making full page replacements unnecessary. The most common library used to achieve this is **pjax** for requesting the HTML snippets, which in turn uses jQuery to place the snippets on the page:

```
var express = require("express")
var app = express()

app.get("/rambo-5", function (req, res) {
  res.send("<p>Rambo 5 is the 5. best movie of the Rambo
series</p>")
})

app.use(express.static(' public' ));

var server = app.listen(3000, function () {
  console.log("App started...")
})
```

The pjax requires the server to send an HTML snippet to be placed on a page as the result for a request in this example. It is just a paragraph tag containing some information about a Rambo movie:

```
<!DOCTYPE html>
<html>
  <head>
    <script src="/jquery.min.js"></script>
    <script src="/jquery.pjax.js"></script>
    <script>
      $(document).ready(function () {
        $(document).pjax(' a' , ' #container' )
        var date = new Date()
        $("#clock").html(date.getHours() + ":" + date.getMinutes()
+ ":" + date.getSeconds())
      })
    </script>

  </head>
  <body>
    <h1>About Rambo</h1>
    <div id="container">
      Go to <a href="/rambo-5">Rambo 5</a>.
```

```
    </div>
    <div>This page rendered at: <span id="clock"></span></div>
  </body>
</html>
```

On the client side, we only need to let pjax highjack all the links inside the container, making it sent a pjax request and insert the appropriate content. The end result is a page that acts like a normal HTML page with links, but the page will not totally refresh on a click. It will just reload the appropriate piece and update the window location.

This approach can be very useful when building server-heavy apps and still being able to maintain a fluid app-like interface without a lot of the build overhead involved in full client-side rendering. Again, we can see a big difference here, making the frontend more of a thin client, therefore this is maybe not a prime candidate for a domain-driven approach, but working closely with a backend build using such an approach because it now is the single source of truth about the application logic in general.

Using JavaScript server side

JavaScript as a language, even though it has been developed for the browser, is not bound to only being executed in a browser context. A browser just naturally contains an environment for the execution of JavaScript in the context of a page. When we want to run JavaScript outside the browser, there is always the option to just execute it directly via a JavaScript engine. There are multiple different engines available, such as **Spidermonkey** from Mozilla or **V8** from Google. Just having JavaScript available is obviously not enough, so we need access to files, sockets, and a multitude of other things to be able to productively work with server-side code.

Node.js has taken over this part, bundling the Google V8 engine with the standard POSIX functions for access to the system-level part. It is by no means the first, there is also **Rhino** from Mozilla, bundling the Java ecosystem with Java for allowing access to all the parts outside the JavaScript standard library:

```
Rhino 1.7 release 5 2015 01 29
js> var file = new java.io.File("./test.txt");
js> importPackage(java.nio.file)
js> Files.readAllLines(file.toPath())
[this is a test text file]
```

The same thing in Node.js looks a little different, and a little bit more like what we expect from JavaScript:

```
> var fs = require("fs")
> fs.readFile("./test.txt", "utf8", function (err, data) {
... if(err) {
..... return console.log(err)
....}
... console.log(data)
..})
> this is a test text file
```

With the basics of interaction being available, we can build complex server-side applications and leverage the nature of server-side development where it makes sense, as we have done throughout the book.

 In the upcoming ECMAScript 6 standard, a new module syntax will be introduced to increase the modularity of JavaScript applications both on the client and server side. ECMAScript 6 is almost finished, but at the time of writing it was not available everywhere. A good source for upcoming changes, and explicitly for the ECMAScript 6 modules, is http://www.2ality.com/2014/09/es6-modules-final.html.

The advantages of a controlled environment

The reason large parts of the book rely on Node.js as the execution environment is the fact that it provides a fixed set of features we can count on. The browser, on the other hand, has always been very flexible and changeable. This is a big advantage when it comes to the development of business applications. As developers, we of course always want to leverage the latest and greatest, and it can make a lot of sense to rely on these technologies where it makes sense, but we also need to be aware of where a stable platform is of a big advantage.

If we want to model the business logic of an application, we hardly count on any new technologies. We need a stable environment where we can execute what we have and what is here to stay. The advantage of JavaScript, of course, is that we can execute on the client and the server side, which means that if we later decide to roll certain logic onto the client side, we can do so, and still fall-back to server-side execution of the rules for verification, if needed.

Advanced modularization

In the past, JavaScript has always been known as the browser language and, for the longest time, loading scripts was outside of the scope of the language itself, but was handled by the HTML part of the environment via script tags.

The rise of more advanced applications on the client side and the rise of server-side JavaScript has changed the language. This is evolving to include a module standard in the next version. For now, there are multiple ways to load other resources and to use one of them is a good idea, what exactly is most likely not important. The important bit here is that loading external modules allows us to better separate our code into logical units, getting away from the 1000+ lines file a lot of the client-side JavaScript programs look like. On the server side, this is a solved problem and the client side is not far behind.

With these different kinds of JavaScript programs and challenges in mind, we can think about what we are aiming for when designing a business application in general and how we have seen domain-driven design take a role in the development process.

The different kinds of complexity

Every business application is faced with different kinds of problems throughout the development. The goal of domain-driven design is to isolate the complexity of an application, making it easy to change and maintain, by providing a language as well as a set of rules for the interaction of objects in the domain.

As we have seen throughout the book, domain-driven design is all about modeling business logic, so it can be accessible for domain experts to judge and evaluate. This is an important part of an application and, if done right, it can save a lot of trouble throughout the development cycle. When driving an application through domain-driven design, we need to identify the core domain and its subdomains. Depending on what our domain is about, the pure business complexity that is there to model is, not the only complexity so.

Neither is every application complex for the business rules, nor does every application lend itself nicely to being modeled in an object-oriented approach like we've seen throughout. There are complexities that are of a different nature, more often closer to what the hard computer science thinks about as its core problem domain, and as with every domain it has its specific ways to talk and model those parts very, clearly and we should use this as well when we come across it.

Making computer science another business domain is a way of abstracting away the intricacies that we come across when dealing with computer science problems. More often than not, trying to expose these problems to the business domain itself is not useful and will lead to more confusion. We can think about computer-science related topics just as a core we interact with to solve very specific problems and develop it as such if we want to isolate it.

Algorithmic complexity

In mathematics and computer science, an algorithm (i/ˈælgərɪðəm/ AL-gə-ri-dhəm), is a self-contained step-by-step set of operations to be performed.

– Wikipedia

At their core, all the things we do can be described as algorithms. They may be very short and very unique, but they are a sequence of steps nonetheless. We have encountered algorithms in our business applications as a sequence of steps that have to take place to initiate the prisoner transport, for example. The algorithms we encountered are business rules, and best modeled as part of the domain itself since they involve the domain objects directly. However, there are other algorithms that we may reuse from mathematics or computer science that are more abstract and therefore don't fit well in the business domain.

When we talk about algorithmic complexity, we most often refer to well-known algorithms such as tree-searching or algorithmic data structures such as lists or skip-lists. These kind of abstract ideas don't lend themselves well to fitting into the domain we are modeling, but are somewhere outside. When we encounter a problem in the domain and it is well served by a known algorithm, we should take advantage of that fact and not muddy the domain with such knowledge but keep it separate.

There are applications, which are bound to have a high algorithmic complexity, and these are most likely not prime candidates for domain-driven design. An example for this may be search, where a lot of knowledge resides in the data structures making searching efficient and therefore useable on a larger scale. The important idea is that in such domains, the business experts are the developers and we should treat the domain in such a way that the developers can communicate best. The most fundamental idea stays the same—that we may want to foster communication through common terms, but in such a case, the common terms are developer specific, and the best way to express it is in code, so the approach is to write code and try it out.

Logical complexity

Another field closely related to algorithmic problems is logical problems. Depending on the domain, these can appear frequently and with a varying degree of complexity. A good example for such problems are configurators of any type, for example, an application allowing you to order a car involves the problem that the extras can conflict. Depending on how many different extras and conflicts there are, the problem can get out of hand quickly.

In logical programming, we state facts and let the engine derive possible solutions for us:

```
var car = new Car()
var configurator = new Configurator(car)

configurator.bodyType(BodyTypes.CONVERTIBLE)
configurator.engine(Engines.V6)
configurator.addExtra(Extras.RADIO)
configurator.addExtra(Extras.GPS)

configurator.errors() // => {conflicts: [{ "convertible": "v6" }]}
```

In the preceding example, the configurator is backed by a rules engine, which allows it to determine potential conflicts in the configuration and reports them back to the user. For this to work, we create a list of facts or constraints:

```
configurator.engineConstraints = [
new Contstraint(BodyTypes.CONVERTIBLE, Engines.V8, Engines.V6_6L)
]
```

With this, a rules engine can check if the constraints are satisfied when we want to order the car.

Solving logical problems in applications is similar to algorithmic ones, best suited for a separate system built for that purpose, exposing a domain-specific logical language to express the problem clearly in logical terms, which is then wrapped in the domain.

The business rules

As we develop the business software, the complexities we are faced with most often are the business rules defined by the clients to which we develop the software. The complexity in these rules often does not stem from the fact that the rule itself has a high complexity, but the fact that the rules are not set in stone and the behavior can change. More importantly, it needs to change quickly to keep the software relevant for the business.

Implementing business rules means tracking what the business needs to do, and this is more often than not based on facts in the head of the business domain experts. The important part of modeling the domain is extracting this knowledge, and verifying its validity with the business as a whole. This is the area where a solid domain model strives to make a difference.

When we are able to talk about the domain with the person who understands the domain best, we can verify quickly, and if we share a common language with this person, he or she can quickly explain to us new rules going forward. Often, complex data structures and algorithms are not the central part of building, such as an application, these pieces can be optimized by an external providing system, the understanding and flexible modeling of the domain is the power of a domain model.

The domains suitable for domain-driven design

Throughout this book, we focused on building a business application, which in essence makes sure we don't over or under book our dungeon, and more specifically to manage the transfer of prisoners that need to be moved due to the constraints of the dungeon. We, as developers, had to rely heavily on the domain experts guiding us through the development, as we don't have the necessary knowledge of the business domain, yet. In this kind of scenario, the establishment of a language comes in very handy as it allows us to talk in a precise manner about what the problems are and how we can deal with new rules, from then on.

Previously, we have seen that not all domains lend themselves nicely to such a strategy, and even domains that do may contain parts that are best handled by secondary systems. Especially when starting out with a new project, we cannot be sure if it makes sense to invest in a heavy domain layer or not.

Banking applications

A domain that is well specified, has a fixed ruleset, and is largely dealing with number should be a prime candidate for being served by well-developed software, so why is there not much accounting software out there, and why are the banks investing so heavily in their development teams?

A lot of people explore accounting problems from a domain-driven perspective, and the problems arise around similar areas. The first is the set of rules, even though the rules seem well defined from the outside, they contain a lot of edge cases that need to be covered, and covered correctly, as, by its nature, large amounts of money are moving through the system. These rules are largely known by a set of experts whose job it is to adjust them every time a change in market makes it necessary. This brings us to the second problem, a lot of very subtle changes need to be expressed and kept consistent across the system.

So, even though on the surface it seems that a relational database covers a lot of the cases in a banking application, the required agility for change and the intrinsic need for a lot of communication with banking experts makes banking a good candidate for applications following domain-driven design, if they indeed want to start a new development.

Banking is one of those domains better left to the experts. If there is no need to build your own accounting system, it's better to buy one of the shelf as the domain complexity and probability for error is very high.

Travel applications

Throughout the book, we have been following a domain related to another prime candidate for domain-driven design, travel, and related booking management. Comparing a dungeon to a hotel may seem a little weird, but from a software point of view, the management is similar. We are trying to manage over- and underbooking while at the same time optimizing revenue.

Booking hotels is one of those domains that seem simple and well-defined on the surface, but are prone to many adjustments and complex rules when digging deeper. It will, for example, be quite easy to completely avoid overbooking when looking at database entries appropriately, but then again, this goes against the goal of maximizing revenue for our hotel. There is a certain amount of overbooking required for compensating the eventual dropping-out of guests.

This is not the only complex part of managing bookings, an important part of the business is adjusting to the season and the current market situation. Booking a hotel while a tradeshow is in town can be significantly more expensive than on a regular day, especially if not booked for the entire duration of the tradeshow since this would mean a room might stay empty even though it could have been booked easily when it was available for the entire timespan. On the other hand, partner discounts can make booking during these shows cheaper again for certain people, and we want to make sure that a certain amount of rooms are available for these people when booking other guests. All bookings also have multiple timelines that need to be managed, such as discount windows, refund windows, and more.

What makes travel even more interesting for domain-driven design, in recent years, is that the representation evolves a lot as well. While previously the systems were optimized to be worked by phone or by a small amount of booking agents, they started to be exposed to the general public via the web. This exposure led to a significant increase in requests and also increased the support needed. Even more recently, the systems are no longer operated directly, but needed to be accessible via APIs to be integrated into search engines.

All this makes travel complex, and way more than a store and load action from the database; especially, since the integration of many systems in combination with general public access puts a huge burden on the developed system's ability to grow and scale, not only in their performance, but more importantly in their complexity.

The domain prerequisites

The domains we have been looking at all involve different forms of complexity in the business areas that are served well using a domain-driven design approach. In the previous sections, we have seen a couple of domains suited well to this approach. What do they have in common?

As seen before, it is all about the different forms of complexity we need to approach. A domain that is moving fast in its business rule set needs more attention toward its modeling because rules need to be adjusted as they evolve. Even more importantly, evolving rules mean that the developers don't have a complete understanding of the rules, so the business experts need to be involved heavily. This means that the language we are building in domain-driven design pays off quickly. Therefore, one important part of domain-driven design is that it is about developer access and the ability to understand the domain. We want to be able to quickly get business experts integrated in the process to avoid misunderstanding. The business experts, in the end, are the ones who drive the domain. We, as developers, provide the software that allows the business to be more successful at what it does. As a part of our domain-driven design approach, we identified what really matters to the business now and how it can be made more efficient and less error-prone.

Approaching the problem from the other side now, and still considering access, means access to the system from other systems needs to be simple. At the moment, this is true for a lot of domains with new devices being popular all the time and business in general driving towards a higher level of integration in a business-to-business environment. How does domain-driven design fit in there? The key again is access. We want to be able to provide multiple interfaces that are accessible from the outside, with the same underlying logic. In domain-driven design, we are all about building a strong service layer, and this layer can then be exposed to different systems via different interfaces without the need to duplicate logic, which will inherently risk a divergence of the parts and logic.

Further reading

As the name of this book suggests, it is already heavily influenced by the ideas Eric Evans presented in his book *Domain-Driven Design: Tackling Complexity in the Heart of Software, Addison-Wesley,* and I would recommend this as a follow-up. He goes in to much more detail about the general approach by providing different examples and from the perspective of a classic Java backend approach.

Another book that should not be missing in any follow-up about software design is, of course, *Patterns of Enterprise Application Architecture, Martin Fowler, Addison-Wesley,* which follows most of the patterns used every day in object-oriented development and goes into more detail about the patterns in general. The book leans more heavily on the Java side, but as we have seen throughout this book, using JavaScript in an object-oriented way is very possible and will be recommended in a lot of the modeling scenarios.

Summary

With applications written in JavaScript becoming more and more complex, the need for stronger application design has increased. Browser applications are growing, and the business reliance on them grows as well. Due to this, what used to be a domain of backend development starts to become important in frontend development. For a long time now, people have been evolving the way backend applications can be modeled for flexibility, so they can grow with the business, and now browser applications need to do the same. There is a lot to learn from the approaches that have been developed over the years, and even though some are not directly transferable to JavaScript, or might not even be needed, the general ideas port over very well. I hope I was able to present some of these ideas throughout the book.

On the other hand, with the rise and adoption of Node.js as a platform for application development, JavaScript has moved into the backend as well, and the same challenges that needed solving for Java or Ruby on the Rails backend systems, now need to be solved for JavaScript/Node.js. It is important to stay true to the nature of JavaScript, as with Node.js, the goal often is to make systems simpler and easier to manage in smaller chunks. This in turn means that a Node.js backend takes a lighter modeling approach than a classic enterprise Java system would have. This is empowering to the developers, as the overarching large-scale architecture discussions move toward a more practical approach being built bottom-up. This should not mean that architecture is not important, but with the split of complexity between frontend and backend systems, the complexity can be managed better with a lighter approach.

Index

V

value objects
about 91, 152, 153
advantages 92, 93
referential transparency 94, 95

W

web application
building 10
dungeon, loading 12
glueing, via express 14, 15
model, creating 12
moving 15, 16
page, displaying 13
route 12

Thank you for buying
JavaScript Domain-Driven Design

About Packt Publishing

Packt, pronounced 'packed', published its first book, *Mastering phpMyAdmin for Effective MySQL Management*, in April 2004, and subsequently continued to specialize in publishing highly focused books on specific technologies and solutions.

Our books and publications share the experiences of your fellow IT professionals in adapting and customizing today's systems, applications, and frameworks. Our solution-based books give you the knowledge and power to customize the software and technologies you're using to get the job done. Packt books are more specific and less general than the IT books you have seen in the past. Our unique business model allows us to bring you more focused information, giving you more of what you need to know, and less of what you don't.

Packt is a modern yet unique publishing company that focuses on producing quality, cutting-edge books for communities of developers, administrators, and newbies alike. For more information, please visit our website at www.packtpub.com.

About Packt Open Source

In 2010, Packt launched two new brands, Packt Open Source and Packt Enterprise, in order to continue its focus on specialization. This book is part of the Packt Open Source brand, home to books published on software built around open source licenses, and offering information to anybody from advanced developers to budding web designers. The Open Source brand also runs Packt's Open Source Royalty Scheme, by which Packt gives a royalty to each open source project about whose software a book is sold.

Writing for Packt

We welcome all inquiries from people who are interested in authoring. Book proposals should be sent to author@packtpub.com. If your book idea is still at an early stage and you would like to discuss it first before writing a formal book proposal, then please contact us; one of our commissioning editors will get in touch with you.

We're not just looking for published authors; if you have strong technical skills but no writing experience, our experienced editors can help you develop a writing career, or simply get some additional reward for your expertise.

Functional Programming in JavaScript

ISBN: 978-1-78439-822-4   Paperback: 172 pages

Unlock the powers of functional programming hidden within JavaScript to build smarter, cleaner, and more reliable web apps

1. Discover what functional programming is, why it's effective, and how it's used in JavaScript.

2. Understand and optimize JavaScript's hidden potential as a true functional language.

3. Explore the best coding practices for real-world applications.

Mastering JavaScript Design Patterns

ISBN: 978-1-78398-798-6   Paperback: 290 pages

Discover how to use JavaScript design patterns to create powerful applications with reliable and maintainable code

1. Learn how to use tried and true software design methodologies to enhance your Javascript code.

2. Discover robust JavaScript implementations of classic as well as advanced design patterns.

3. Packed with easy-to-follow examples that can be used to create reusable code and extensible designs.

Please check **www.PacktPub.com** for information on our titles

Object-Oriented JavaScript

Second Edition

ISBN: 978-1-84969-312-7   Paperback: 382 pages

Learn everything you need to know about OOJS in this comprehensive guide

1. Think in JavaScript.

2. Make object-oriented programming accessible and understandable to web developers.

3. Apply design patterns to solve JavaScript coding problems.

JavaScript Testing Beginner's Guide

ISBN: 978-1-84951-000-4   Paperback: 272 pages

Test and debug JavaScript the easy way

1. Learn different techniques to test JavaScript, no matter how long or short your code might be.

2. Discover the most important and free tools to help make your debugging task less painful.

3. Discover how to test user interfaces that are controlled by JavaScript.

Please check **www.PacktPub.com** for information on our titles

24240228R00117

Made in the USA
San Bernardino, CA
17 September 2015